EMPOWERED FOR EXPLOIT

A LIFE-CHANGING 30 DAY PRAYER MANUAL WITH FASTING

AMOS FENWA

EMPOWERED FOR EXPLOIT

Copyright © January 2024 by **AMOS FENWA**

ISBN - 9798876638885

All rights reserved.

Unless otherwise indicated, all Scripture quotations in this volume are from the King James Version of the Bible.

Published by:
Amos Fenwa Ministries
Solution Arena, 156, Ikorodu Road
Onipanu Bus Stop, Lagos.
08125113314, 08033387124,
07037276477

This mini-book is designed for the annual 30-day prayer programme of HOLYGHOST CHRISTIAN CENTRE.
It is advisable to include fasting along with the prayer in order to get maximum result. You can add your own prayer point on each day of the prayer schedule.

MAY GOD ANSWER ALL YOUR PRAYERS!

- AMOS FENWA

CONTENTS

DAY 1 - SPIRITUAL DETOXIFICATION
DAY 2 - AN OPENED EYES AND HEARING EAR
DAY 3 - DIVINE CLEANSING BY THE HOLY GHOST
DAY 4 - ACTIVATING IRRESISTIBLE FAVOR
DAY 5 - I WILL LIVE
DAY 6 - DEFEATING ANCESTRAL YOKES
DAY 7 - I SHALL BE REMEMBERED THIS YEAR
DAY 8 - RECOVERING MISSED OPPORTUNITIES
DAY 9 - PRAYER FOR THE BODY OF CHRIST AND HCC WORLDWIDE
DAY 10 - OPENED HEAVENS
DAY 11 - LET MY FINANCIAL GATE OPEN
DAY 12 - HEAVEN CONSCIOUSNESS
DAY 13 - VICTORY OVER THE SPIRIT OF DEPRESSION

INTRODUCTION

Daniel 11:32 "*Those who do wickedly against the covenant he shall corrupt with flattery;* **but the people who know their God shall be strong, and carry out great exploits."(NKJV)**

Without any doubt, it's quite evident and clear as crystals that Jesus Christ is the end of the law. If these three men: Daniel, Joseph and Job could do great exploits in their generation with their impact written in the sand of time and are still recognized till date, how much more we, New Testament believers; saved and living under the grace to do greater exploits? Do we fully know the God we serve? Many believers have become burdens and objects of mockery due to their lack of adequate knowledge about the God they serve. You see, God will never reveal nor manifest himself to you beyond the level of your spiritual knowledge and understanding about Him.

When you are not knowledgeable in the things of God, it will be difficult for Him to communicate with you. For example, Samuel as a young boy was dedicated to serve God under Eli the priest but When God wanted to reveal Himself to the boy, he could not discern the voice of God from that of Eli. So, Eli had to tutor him.

1 Samuel 3:7-8 *"Now Samuel did not yet know the LORD, nor had the word of the LORD yet been revealed to him. So the LORD called Samuel again for the third time. And he arose and went to Eli and said, "Here I am, for you called me." Then Eli discerned that the LORD was calling the boy."* (NASB)

If you see God as the mightiest, best believe that He will reveal Himself as such in your life. On the other hand, if you see him with the limitation of your eyes and mind, you will experience only a limited version of God.

The men of old knew him as unlimited and incomparable and He revealed himself to them as such. Hallelujah! I am glad to let you know that you are enriched and empowered without limits to do greater exploits beyond Daniel, Joseph and

Job. Christ has perfected all on our behalf, all we have to do is engage faith in exploring the great riches of the Kingdom. The exploration process is the spiritual search of mystery and knowledge towards development and growth in Christ. Whatever you can imagine within yourself, believe through faith that you will have it because it's your birthright in God.

What does it mean to do exploit?
To do exploit typically refers to performing notable achievements or remarkable actions, often in a skillful or daring manner. *"...But the people who know their God shall be strong, and carry out great exploits"*. **Daniel 11:32b**

In the second part of the anchor scripture of Daniel 11, verse 32, exploit is used in the context of performing achievements through God and by God. Littered throughout scriptures are men and women who did exploits for God —there was Gideon and his 300 soldiers **(Judges 7:19-23)**, Elijah on Mount Carmel **(1 Kings 18:36-39)**, Samson **(Judges 14:5-6)**, the apostles who were martyred for the sake of the gospel; one who stands out the most being Apostle Paul and all the heroes of faith as mentioned in Hebrews 11.

Before we delve into what it means and takes to do exploits, it is important that we are armed with the right knowledge and information about the season we are stepping into.

CHAPTER ONE

WHAT IS FASTING?

Fasting is one of the most important spiritual practices in the Christian faith. It is indeed an open secret because Jesus after being baptized at the Jordan River by John the Baptist and after the dramatic announcement from Heaven by the Holy Spirit that He pleased God; the next thing He did prior to starting His earthly ministry was to engage in 40-Day and Night period of fasting in the wilderness which is called Dry Fast. Fasting, therefore, is the practice of chastising your flesh by abstaining from food and natural pleasures for a selected period of time while focusing on a deeper relationship with God.

Why Fast?

There are quite a number of reasons for going on a fast. A few of them are listed below:

- To get clear direction for the year
- For spiritual growth in our lives

- To obtain personal breakthroughs
- To see the supernatural hand of God released in our churches
- To protect and preserve our children in the educational system and society
- For financial breakthroughs
- For enrichment in the covenant relation of marriages
- For our Country's Leaders and the President to do God's will.

The enemy of our souls does everything in his power to hinder our understanding and the practice of fasting with prayer. If you are probably wondering why this should be the case you already could figure it out. Satan knows that we will have spiritual power if we engage in fasting as a congruent part of our spiritual walk. It makes us discipline our body to bow to the Spirit. If we are to be successful in the practice of faith and we call ourselves followers of Jesus we must engage in the spiritual discipline of fasting through some forms and measures. After Jesus returned to heaven, the early church continued fasting with prayer as a habitual practice.

TYPES OF FAST

1.   Dry fast

No food, water and denying self of pleasure over 24 hours period.

Moses, Elijah and Paul practiced this kind of fast. (Exodus 34:28, 1 Kings 19:8, Acts 9:9)

2.   Normal fast

Not eating food or drinking liquid till noon or evening.

3.   Partial fast

This involves taking just an insignificant quantity and quality of food, rather than your usual portions otherwise known as Daniel fast.

WHEN FASTING IS IN VAIN

Telltale signs of fasting going the wrong way are when;

1.   Your prayer is very shallow
2.   You cannot study the Bible
3.   You hold malice and find it difficult to forgive
4.   You spitefully eat or drink water
5.   You make unnecessary jest of others

6. You hate to give your substance to God or the needy
7. You devote yourself to another thing completely
8. Your mind is not fixed in the fasting exercise
9. You fornicate during or after fasting
10. You commit adultery at will
11. You speak lies instead of the truth
12. You curse people when irritated

So, there's more to fasting beyond skipping food and drinks. Your outright behaviour and disposition must align with the spirit all the time.

BENEFITS OF FASTING

Many may not be conversant with the inherent benefits of fasting, nevertheless, there are long established blessing arising from fasting. Whatever we do towards God cannot be in vain.

Isaiah 45:19 *"I have not spoken in secret, In a dark place of the earth; I did not say to the seed of Jacob, 'Seek Me in vain'; I, the LORD, speak righteousness, I declare things that are right."* **(NKJV)**

While I am sure that many more benefits exist for fasting with prayer, here are the top ten benefits from the scriptures.

1. **Receiving power to overcome Satan and his minions**

In Matthew 4:1-11, Jesus put Satan in his place when he was tempted in the wilderness for an extended period of time. In verse 11 we read *"Then the devil left Him, and behold, angels came and ministered to Him."* Luke, the physician, writes in Luke 4:13 *"Now when the devil had ended every temptation, he departed from Him until an opportune time."* If you want the devil to leave you alone for seasons since he is a pest, the best thing to do is to take up a habitual life of prayer and fasting. When he returns for another bout, you will no doubt be ready to defeat him.

2.　Preparation for the work of God

The Lord Jesus did not begin ministry work until after a 40-day fasting period. This is not to say everyone must fast for 40 days to serve God. No! The scriptures are clear with examples of many kinds of fasts. May the Spirit lead you to what is appropriate for you. (Luke 4:1-13)

3.　Hearing clearly what the will of God is about any matter

God can speak to us at any time regardless of whether we are fasting or not. However, we must remember that we are engaged in spiritual warfare and sometimes the battle is so fierce, reinforcements are needed. Daniel fasted for 21 days and found out from a visiting angel that a demon prince had resisted him for those 21 days. The angel had pertinent information for Daniel which could have been aborted but for his persistence in prayer and fasting. We still read those inspiring prophetic words till today. And if it was good for Daniel, it will work for us.

4.   Petitioning Heaven for God's will to come to pass

We are told in Luke 2:36 that a woman called Anna who lived in the temple for years *"served God with fastings night and day."* This woman with a prophetic anointing came by when baby Jesus was being dedicated in the Temple. According to verse 38, *"And coming in that instant she gave thanks to the Lord, and spoke of Him to all those who looked for redemption in Jerusalem."*

5.   Offering Sacrifice to God that delights Him

Paul writes in Romans 12:1 *"I beseech you therefore, brethren, by the mercies of God, that you present your bodies a living sacrifice, holy, acceptable to God, which is your reasonable service."* I expanded this concept in an article titled "Fasting as a living sacrifice" which explains both the health and spiritual benefits of fasting.

6.   For Intercession

Acts 27 gives an account of when Paul the Apostle in the company of Roman soldiers and some people were on a ship heading to Rome. At one point a tempestuous wind called Euroclydon eventually led to a shipwreck on the Island of Malta. The story of their deliverance from the very difficult situation of enduring several days of darkness having been lost at sea was divine providence. Paul spent time fasting with prayer petitioning the Lord of Heaven for the lives on the ship and he heard from Heaven that no life will be lost (Acts 27:22-26). He said *"there stood by me this night an Angel of the God to Whom I belong and Whom I serve."*

7.   For enduring covenants with God

Spiritual fasting is a sacrifice in itself and God says that His saints enter into a covenant with Him when they make a sacrifice. God decides the details and terms of the covenant. This spiritual principle applies to any type of sacrifice God asks of us. Read Psalm 50:23. I write a bit more about this in an article titled "Fasting as a living sacrifice."

8. Fasting humbles and changes you

One of the most effective ways to humble yourself is through fasting. There is something about having food that causes us as humans to get carried away. It is interesting that the problem in the garden with Adam and Eve began with food as we read from Genesis 3. Intentional abstinence from the pleasure of one or more meals has a miraculous way of humbling us causing a repentant posture. If your abstinence is not intentional you will get angry quickly at the slightest provocation. In Psalm 35:13 David said, *"I humbled my soul with fasting…"*

9. It brings deliverance for a troubled nation

When Hamman tried to destroy the Jews in the Assyrian Kingdom, Esther fasted for three days along with her maidens. God intervened mightily, saving them and destroying their enemies. Read the book of Esther. It is a book where you won't find the word God mentioned however everything in it screams "God is in control."

10.   Promotes Healthy body

It has been found by medical researchers that fasting even if it does not include prayer (non-spiritual fast) has several health benefits. Has the Lord been speaking to you about fasting? Are you afraid or just lazy? Maybe knowing what you stand to benefit yourself and God's Kingdom as a whole will spur you on. Take intentional baby steps and He will meet you where you are. He is indeed faithful.

More power to you today and always in Jesus' name.

Here are a few tips to help you in this period of consecration:

1.   Focus on the Word of God and increase prayer during a fast.

2.   Fasting will increase your faith and your relationship with God.

3.   During a fast, prayers must be specific. It is wise to keep a journal of your prayers and how God answers them.

4.   Avoid eating a large meal before you begin to fast. This will make you even hungrier when you start your fast. Continue to eat fruit and vegetables for at least three days before you begin to fast.

5.   Drink lots of water and fluids: bottled, distilled, or purified water should be warm at room temperature. Do not drink tap water.

6.   Day one will be the hardest day of the fast, each day actually gets easier as you pray and press your way into God.

7.   Fasting strengthens your inner will. You will not starve to death by fasting. Fast until God has dealt with you or you feel a release.

8.   Fasting will not impair your health; however, consult with your physician if you have any concerns. It is not recommended that a pregnant woman should fast.

9.   Headaches, bad breath, nausea and rundown feelings are signs that the fast is working. These symptoms should cease after the 3rd day.

10.   The victory often comes after the fast is over.

11.   Wisdom should be used when breaking a fast. Do not eat food like meats that are hard to digest when breaking a fast. Eat fruits or vegetables and drink plenty of water before, during and after fasting.

CHAPTER THREE

WHAT DOES IT MEAN TO DO EXPLOIT?

This study is based upon the last part of Daniel 11:32 as it is recorded in the King James Version. Three ideas are contained in this verse. We have the triangular thought of *knowing God, being strong* and *doing exploits.* God's people are characterized by what they know, what they are and what they do. Believers (Christians) are different from worldly and unconverted people in these three respects — in the matter of *knowing, being* and *doing.* Notice that these three characteristics of the child of God are related, for only as we know God can we be strong; and only as we are strong can we undertake exploits in the name of the Lord. Conversely, if we are not doing exploits for God, it is because we are not strong; and if we are not strong it is because we do not know God well enough. In this study we shall examine the three ideas of Daniel 11:32.

1. KNOWING GOD

It is not enough to know about Him. We must truly know Him. It is possible to know much about the Lord, His nature and attributes, and yet not to know Him personally. We can, of course, only come to know God through the Lord Jesus Christ. The scripture records Jesus saying in John 14:6 *"Jesus answered, "I am the way, the truth, and the life. The only way to the Father is through me"*; there are a few scriptures to corroborate this (see Job 22:21, John 17:3).

This is the *initial* sense in which we come to know God as our loving heavenly Father through faith in the Lord Jesus Christ as our Saviour; but we must go on to know Him *progressively*, for there are degrees of knowing Him. The scripture says in Philippians 3:10 *"All I want is to know Christ and the power that raised him from death. I want to share in his sufferings and be like him even in his death"*. (Also see John 14:9). This begs the question: How do we really get to know God?

■ *We get to know Him as we spend time in communion and in fellowship with Him:* We can only really get to know anyone by spending time in his or her presence, and we can only really get to know God as we spend time alone with Him and cultivate fellowship and friendship with Him — as *Enoch* did in Genesis 5:22-24.

■ *We get to know Him as we listen to Him speaking to us:* When friends get together, they talk and listen to one another, and thus they get to know one another; and as we wait in the presence of God regularly, He speaks to us in and through His Word, and we hear His voice and, like Mary, really come to know Him (Luke 10:38-42).

■ *We get to know Him by speaking to Him:* Fellowship is mutual. It is not a one-sided affair, and when we come into the presence of the Lord and open our hearts and our lips to Him we get to know Him, as David did (Psalm 55:16-17); and as Daniel did. Daniel 6:10 *'Now when Daniel knew that the writing was signed, he went into his house; and his windows being open in his chamber toward Jerusalem, he kneeled upon his knees three times a day, and prayed, and gave thanks before his God, as he did aforetime."*

■ *We get to know Him by observing His ways of working:* We get to know God as we see what He does and how He does it, and in this respect, we can only get to know Him gradually in the daily paths of practical experience as we follow on to know Him. In view of this, let us examine Hosea 6:3 and 2 Peter 3:18.

"Let us acknowledge the LORD; let us press on to acknowledge him. As surely as the sun rises, he will appear; he will come to us like the winter rains, like the spring rains that water the earth." (Hosea 6:3)

"But grow in the grace and knowledge of our Lord and Savior Jesus Christ. To him be the glory both now and to the day of eternity. Amen." (2 Peter 3:18)

These scriptures should stir us to ask the important question: *How much do I know Him?* For the measure of our *knowing* determines the measure of our *being* and our *doing!*

2. BEING STRONG

The more we know Him, the stronger we shall be. What does this mean? Does it mean we shall be strong *physically?* This passage of the Bible does not speak only of physical strength; we cannot negate the fact that He is the source of our physical life as well as of our spiritual life. So, yes! We shall be strong *physically, spiritually and morally*. Just as Daniel was when he was cast into the lions' den and as Shadrach, Meshach and Abednego were when they were cast into the fiery furnace —we shall be strong. The scripture says in Ephesians 6:10 *"Finally, be strong in the Lord and in the strength of his might."*

As we know the Lord:

■ *We become stronger in our confidence in Him*: We shall be filled with a holy assurance; we shall *know* like Job did in Job 19:25. We shall know that everything works together for our good as it is written in Romans 8:28 and we shall know that no matter what comes our way, we shall have confidence in God and His enabling to endure in adversity, trial, sorrow and any kind of affliction. (2 Timothy 1:12)

■ *We become stronger in our power to overcome temptation and evil:* How weak we are sometimes! Why? Because we do not know the Lord enough; but as we get to know Him better, we shall receive more power to meet and to overcome those things that are displeasing to Him. *"But ye shall receive power, after that the Holy Ghost is come upon you: and ye shall be witnesses unto me both in Jerusalem, and in all Judaea, and in Samaria, and unto the uttermost part of the earth."* (Acts 1:8.)

■ ***We shall become stronger in our ability to be a strength to others***. A Christian once prayed, *"Lord, make me as thine arm, upon which the troubled and tried can lean!"* Is that the kind of prayer we should pray and God will answer? Indeed, it is! Thus, as we know God, we become a source of strength to others who are in need of one in this cruel world. (Isaiah 40:28-31).

When we are strong, then what happens? We are able do exploits!

3. DOING EXPLOITS FOR GOD

An exploit is: ***"A heroic deed of achievement"***; a great and daring feat. The Bible is full of illustrations of men and women who did exploits for God. Think of *Gideon* and his 300 men (Judges 7:19-23); *Samson* that tore a lion (Judges 14:5-6); *Elijah on Mount Carmel* (1 Kings 18:36-39); and see God's picture gallery of the *Heroes of Faith* in Hebrews 11. Think also of the *apostles and the early Christians* who hazarded their lives for the name of the Lord (Acts 15:26), and turned the world upside down (Acts 17:6)! If we really know God and are thereby made strong in Him, we also shall do exploits. And this can be in two ways:

1. ***By prayer***: History speaks of men like George Muller and Hudson Taylor, who by prayer alone *"moved the arm that rules the world"*. *"Give me Scotland or I die"* famously came from the lips of John Knox, the Scottish reformer. We cannot successfully do exploits without prayer. It is the engine that our spirits thrive upon in this world.

2. ***By Witnessing***: Our Lord Jesus commands us in Matthew 28:19 to go into the world and preach the gospel. On the list of exploits, this is what tops the list – sharing the Word of God. The Scripture writes of the early Christians whose hearts were so full of the love of Christ that their lips were

constantly filled with the message of the gospel as they went from place to place witnessing to the power and grace of God.

Our Lord Jesus says to us confidently in John 14:12 saying: *"Truly, truly, I say to you, whoever believes in me will also do the works that I do; and greater works than these will he do, because I am going to the Father."*
In view of this, let us do what we are empowered to do as we begin this 30–Day fasting and prayer.

On your mark…. Get Set ….. Go Do Exploits!

DAILY PRAYER SECTION

DAY 1

SPIRITUAL DETOXIFICATION

SCRIPTURE OF THE DAY

1 Corinthians 3:3 *"You are still worldly. For since there is jealousy and quarreling among you, are you not worldly? Are you not acting like mere humans?"*

EXHORTATION

The popular Chinese proverb says the journey of a thousand miles begins with a single step. In my opinion, that is the most important step. As we begin the 30–Day journey of empowerment to do exploits in 2024, there is a need to go through a spiritual detoxification. There is a need to charge our spirits and walk in the Spirit. Many believers still have the works of the flesh on display such as: lying, pride, covetousness, lust, fornication, adultery, fraud, un-forgiveness etc. The reason many find it hard to have a blooming relationship with God is because of their desires to fulfill the promptings of the flesh instead of the Spirit. God cannot be mocked and He knows his own (John 10:27). Your life is a direct reflection of who you submit to - the flesh or the Spirit. In making decisions, it is important to be very careful whose leading we yield to; the flesh or the spirit.

Paul says in Galatians 2:20 *"I am now crucified with Christ; it is not I who live but Christ lives in me"*. This should be our anthem and serve as a reminder as we walk through life with Jesus.

I urge you to submit to the Lord Jesus for cleansing and spiritual detoxification.

CONFESSION

Psalm 51:2 *"Wash me thoroughly from mine iniquity, and cleanse me from my sin." (KJV)*

PRAYER POINTS

1. Lord, break me down in spirit, soul and body and remold me now.
2. Any habit in me hindering my full glory from manifesting, O Lord, give me grace to change it.
3. You spirit behind the works of the flesh in my life, I cast you out!
4. Lord, change me as you did for your servants, Peter and Saul.

5. Lord, show me deep revelations about heaven.
6. Let the Holy Ghost take over my life completely.
7. I shall not end my journey in carnality in Jesus' name.
8. Lord, give me power to overcome my flesh.
9. I silence the voice of flesh speaking over the things of God in my life.
10. My flesh I command you to yield to the calling of the Holy Spirit.
11. I will not be lost in the flesh but be incubated in the spirit of God.
12. Let the sins of my flesh be washed by the blood of Jesus.

DAY 2

AN OPENED EYES AND HEARING EAR

SCRIPTURE OF THE DAY
2 Kings 6:18-20 *"And when they came down to him, Elisha prayed unto the LORD, and said, Smite this people, I pray thee, with blindness. And he smote them with*

blindness according to the word of Elisha. And Elisha said unto them, this is not the way, neither is this the city: follow me, and I will bring you to the man whom ye seek. But he led them to Samaria. And it came to pass, when they were come into Samaria, that Elisha said, LORD, open the eyes of these men that they may see. And the LORD opened their eyes, and they saw; and, behold, they were in the midst of Samaria."

EXHORTATION

God communicates His plans for us, and directs us through our eyes and ears—first, He shows us and then, He does it. When a man's senses are insensitive or lose their function, such a man would be incapacitated to do anything meaningful in a very long time. The absence of light brings chaos and causes stumbling to the feet of whoever walks in it. As we move forward in the year 2024, let's walk in light, discernment and with an active eye and ear. Paying attention to all that God is saying and instructing per time because therein lies your empowerment for exploits! How else can you take hold of all that God has for you when your eyes cannot see and your ears cannot hear? Today and always, be intentional about asking the

Lord to open your eyes daily to all he is doing in your life.

CONFESSION

Daniel 2:22 *"He revealeth the deep and secret things: he knoweth what [is] in the darkness, and the light dwelleth with him."*

PRAYER POINTS

1. Thank God for His gift of vision and dreams.
2. O Lord, revive all my dormant spiritual gifts in Jesus' name.
3. Lord let the anointing to see the will and purpose of God for my life fall upon me.
4. Let every veil covering my spiritual eyes catch fire.
5. Holy Spirit, make my spiritual visions clear and plain in Jesus' name.
6. My Lord, open my eyes to know the secret about my home, marriage, health and business according to your word in Jeremiah 33:3.
7. Every veil over my spiritual vision from the dark kingdom; catch fire .
8. Every power that makes me forget my dreams, be arrested in Jesus' name.

9. Lord, upgrade my spiritual gifts to be sensitive to your signals at all times.
10. Lord, let the Holy Spirit guide me at all times in Jesus' name.
11. Lord, open my spiritual ear to hear your voice from heaven.
12. I bind spiritual deafness as from now on in Jesus' name

DAY 3

DIVINE CLEANSING BY THE HOLY GHOST

SCRIPTURE OF THE DAY

Colossians 2: 14-15 *"Blotting out the handwriting of ordinances that was against us, which was contrary to us, and took it out of the way, nailing it to his cross; And having spoiled principalities and powers, he made a shew of the openly, triumphing over them in it."*

EXHORTATION

Today is the day of repentance. I'd like to urge you to acknowledge the mistakes you have made in the past and the sins you committed greatly against the Lord. Then, approach Him with godly sorrow and deep repentance in your heart, confessing your sins and the sins of your ancestors, following Daniels's godly example in Daniel 9. Daniel was praying for the restoration of Jerusalem. You should follow that model and in place of Jerusalem, substitute your family and your divine destiny. This is such a crucial first step. You must do it slowly, all day and possibly during the night too.

Confess your sins one by one; mention them by name, especially sexual sins. Do not forget the hidden sins of the heart and the chief among them as mentioned in Gal. 5:19-21. Ask God for forgiveness and mercy. Now, believe that the Lord has forgiven you as He has promised in His Word. Please note that the Holy Spirit will remind you of many forgotten sins you fail to confess. You need to repent of them all if you really want to see results in this fasting period.

This is what will set the tone and lay the foundation for the rest of this 30–Day program. It is what will activate divine intervention in every area of your life. The Lord has been waiting a long time for you to get on your knees and do this properly and thoroughly. After thorough repentance (please note that repentance can last for hours) then you will be positioned to renounce your involvement in ungodly associations.

CONFESSION

Galatians 3: 13-14 *"Christ hath redeemed us from the curse of the law, being made a curse for us: for it is written, cursed is everyone that hangs on a tree: That the blessing of Abraham might come on the Gentiles through Jesus Christ; that we might receive the promise of the Spirit through faith."*

PRAYER POINTS

1. Lord, I repent of any sin I have committed knowingly or unknowingly.
2. I ask for your forgiveness. Please wash me clean with the blood of Jesus Christ.
3. Let any sin holding my life bound be nullified by the blood of Jesus.
4. Lord, give me power to stop sinning and pursue righteousness.
5. My flesh, hear the word of God; you are dead to sin and alive unto righteousness.
6. I declare that I will only yield my body to the

righteousness of God.

7. I silence every evil voice speaking against my life from the camp of the wicked by the power in the blood of Jesus.

8. I declare: the blood of Jesus cleanses me from every consequence of my involvement in any sinful and untoward activities.

9. I renounce all curses on my eyes, stomach/womb, body, hands, legs, in Jesus' name.

10. Anything the devil can use to hinder my prayers, Lord let your blood fight it for me.

11. Holy Spirit, I give way to your Spirit in my life in Jesus' name.

12. O Lord, in 2024, my life will give you glory in Jesus' name.

DAY 4

ACTIVATING IRRESISTIBLE FAVOR

SCRIPTURE OF THE DAY

Esther 2:9 "*She pleased him and won his favor. Immediately he provided her with her beauty treatments and special food. He assigned to her seven female attendants* *selected from the king's palace and moved her and her attendants into the best place in the harem."*

EXHORTATION

Esther, an ordinary woman chosen for an extraordinary mission, teaches us valuable lessons about activating irresistible favor in our lives. Her story teaches us to trust in God's timing, to have bold faith and seek God's guidance through prayer and fasting. In this 30–Day journey, we have come to seek God earnestly, spend time in prayer, listen for His voice, and align our hearts with His will.

The scripture speaks of Jesus that He grew in favor with God and with man (Luke 2:52). Favour is someone speaking for you in rooms you cannot ordinarily enter. Favour is when the kings and rulers of nations are being drawn to your light. Favour is enjoying help in different phases of life. In this consecration period, I decree the favor of God in your life and business in Jesus' name.

CONFESSION

Esther 2:15 *"Now when the turn of Esther, the daughter of Abigail the uncle of Mordecai, who had taken* *her for his daughter, was to go in unto the king, she required nothing but what Hegai the king's chamberlain, the keeper of the women, appointed. And Esther obtained favour in the sight of all them that looked upon her."*

PRAYER POINTS

1. Lord, baptize me with the spirit of grace and supplication and favor.

2. I reject the spirit of rejection, disfavor and hatred in Jesus' name.

3. You seed of generational rejection and disfavor, die in my life in Jesus' name.

4. Lord, perfume my life with your oil of favor.

5. Thou favor of God upon my life, begin to displace people for my sake.

6. Favor of God, create strategic vacancies for me wherever I go.

7. Let any foundational spirit of hatred and rejection in my life die right now in Jesus' name.

8. Every seed of witchcraft in my life; die by fire.

9. I command every representation and mark of rejection in my life to burn and perish.

10. Every seed of rejection, hatred and failure in my life, I command you to be consumed by

the fire of God in the name of Jesus.

11. Every curse, spell, jinx, and enchantment of disfavor in my life, whether acquired, inherited, ancestral or environmental, be destroyed from my foundation in Jesus mighty name.

12. Every spirit servicing and enforcing disfavor, rejection and hatred in my life: be bound and be liquidated by God's fire in Jesus name.

DAY 5

I WILL LIVE

SCRIPTURE OF THE DAY

Hosea 13:14 *"I will ransom them from the power of grave; I will redeem them from death: O death, I will be thy plagues; O grave, I will be thy destruction: repentance shall be hid from mine eyes."* **(KJV)**

EXHORTATION

Year after year, people die untimely. The grave side is full of aborted dreams, unfinished projects, unfulfilled purpose, unleashed destinies and the brains containing some of the greatest innovations yet known to man. For us, God's children, the promise of God to us is long life and He keeps His promises always! He has a track record of faithfulness. Our safety is in Jesus. We have received the life of Christ, a life above death —an eternal life.

The devil is a roaring lion that goes about attacking the lives of God's children, oppressing them with all kinds of things, cutting lives short. Yet, our God is greater and is the final authority. Absolutely no man has the right to end your life or determine how long you should live. God is the giver of life and as you engage in the prayer points in this booklet, every programme of death shall be canceled over you and your loved ones in Jesus' name.

CONFESSION:
Psalms 91:16 *"With long life will I satisfy him, and shew him my salvation."*
Psalm 118:17 *"I shall not die, but live, and declare the works of the LORD."*

PRAYER POINTS
1.   I revoke now by the blood of Jesus every

sentence of death passed upon me and my loved ones in the marine, occult and witchcraft kingdoms.

2. I command any sentence of death against me and my loved ones to backfire by fire in Jesus' name.

3. Every man or woman planning my death shall die in place of me this year.

4. I command every coffin prepared for me by my enemies to catch fire and be roasted to ashes now.

5. I command every death before my divinely appointed time to be cancelled in Jesus' name.

6. Let every curse of death hanging on my head be broken by the blood of Jesus.

7. I cancel every arrow of premature death in the remaining days of this year in Jesus' name.

8. I command any coffin or grave that has swallowed my wealth, health, children, money, business and ministry to open and vomit them by fire now.

9. I refuse to bury any of my children and loved ones this year in Jesus' name.

10. I declare the release of my marriage, husband, wife and children from the cage and grave of the coffin spirit now by fire.

11. Every door of death opened before me and my family, waiting for us to walk right in; I shut you up permanently in the name of Jesus.

12. The promises of long life as spoken to me by God are established in my life and in my home in Jesus' name.

DAY 6

DEFEATING ANCESTRAL YOKES

SCRIPTURE OF THE DAY

Isaiah 9:4 *"For You have broken the yoke of his burden And the staff of his shoulder, The rod of his oppressor, As in the day of Midian."* (NKJV)

EXHORTATION

There are different kinds of enemies or foes a man may have. You can have current foes, past foes, future foes, and ancient foes. The ancient foes are difficult to battle, so today's topic falls into that area. The Bible says *"The fathers have eaten sour grapes, And the children's teeth are set on edge."* (Jeremiah 31:29-30).

What is a yoke?

- The yoke is an instrument of toil in the farmland.
- The yoke suggests blood and sweat.
- Yokes are deadly destroyers of destiny.
- Yokes are tormentors and terminators.
- Yokes are robbers taking away pleasures and increasing pressure.
- Yokes are afflictions that are too difficult to personally break and too heavy to bear.
- A yoke is anything that puts a limitation or destruction upon one's life.
- Yoke is any hold of demonic force upon a life. So, it binds, it breaks, it bites, it burns, it brings destruction and limitation.
- Yokes are demonic additions to make man's life miserable.

Every yoke, as far as the bible is concerned; can only be destroyed by the anointing. Not by drinking salty water, not by being whipped in a church, not by going to have your bath at the beach, not by throwing your clothes into the rivers, not by celebrating demonic parties – all yokes can only be broken by the anointing.

Ancestral powers are evil powers of your father's house, family tree demons, powers of an inherited idol. They are powers assigned to punish a family or to extend a curse on a family. They are foundational powers that have been worshiped by the ancestors particularly in ancient times.

The miracle about praying this prayer is this: when these kinds of prayer are properly executed — prayed with fire, with power, with passion, with force, with violence, and with faith, there is bound to be an avalanche of testimonies to follow.

CONFESSION

Isaiah 10:27 *"It shall come to pass in that day That his burden will be taken away from your shoulder, And his yoke from your neck, And the yoke will be destroyed because of the anointing oil."* (NKJV)

PRAYER POINTS

1. Jesus Christ the Yoke breaker; I'm available, break my yoke now in Your holy name.
2. Powers that stopped my ancestors, you cannot stop me; die in the name of Jesus.
3. Any power that must die for my life to move forward; die in the name of Jesus.

4. Powers dragging me backward, you're a liar; die in the name of Jesus.

5. By the blood of Jesus, I terminate every long-time bondage troubling my life.

6. Any curse of delay, operating in my root; break in the name of Jesus.

7. My parent's shoes and garment of suffering shall not fit me in the name of Jesus.

8. Every satanic tree in my family catch fire in the name of Jesus.

9. Blood of Jesus, heal my family foundation today in the name of Jesus.

10. The spiritual umbilical cord, tying me to hardship through ancestral powers, die in the name of Jesus (touch your belly button while praying this prayer)

11. My Father, you are my glory and the lifter of my head; lift my head in the name of Jesus.

12. The Lord God of Elijah, arise; let my enemies destroy themselves, in the name of Jesus!

DAY 7

I SHALL BE REMEMBERED THIS YEAR

SCRIPTURE OF THE DAY

Genesis 8:1 "And God remembered Noah, and every living thing, and all the cattle that were with him in the ark: and God made a wind to pass over the earth, and the waters assuaged;"

EXHORTATION

God has a plan for every creature. But when His promise and plan is getting delayed, we can call on Him to remember us. We can provoke His remembrance by our prayer, fasting, giving and through service to him.

The entertainment of Angels by Abraham provoked the pronouncement of Angel concerning the promised child Isaac. Genesis 21:1 *"And the Lord visited Sarah as he had said, and the Lord did unto Sarah as he had spoken"*. When you seem forgotten in life by God, it is certain that you will not be remembered by man. Why? He uses men to get His will fulfilled on the earth. Stagnation, barrenness, delay in marriage, poverty are indications of not being remembered.

Like Mordecai, you shall be remembered. It was said of Esther in *Esther 6:1 "On that night could not the king sleep, and he commanded to bring the book of records of the chronicles; and they were read before the king."*

You shall be remembered in Jesus' name.

CONFESSION

Jeremiah 29:11 "For I know the thoughts that I think toward you, saith the LORD, thoughts of peace, and not of evil, to give you an expected end."

PRAYER POINTS

1. Lord, open the book of remembrance before me this month.
2. Anointing for pleasant surprises, fall upon me now.
3. Doors of new things shall be opened unto me and my family members.
4. Lord, exceed my expectations in the remaining months of this year.

5. All hanging prophecies over my head, be fulfilled now.
6. Lord, raise help from unknown quarters this year for me.
7. Foundational powers sitting on my destiny and dreams for this year, I overthrow you by the power of God.
8. Powers renewing the bondage of non-achievement, hear the word of God, die, die, die.
9. My Goals for this year shall be actualized by fire.
10. I command divine remembrance from all the four corners of the world.
11. I prophesy this year shall favor me. All that is designed for me to achieve this year, may it be orchestrated by heaven.
12. Rachel was remembered and her womb opened; Lord remember me today and make me fruitful.

DAY 8

RECOVERING MISSED OPPORTUNITIES

SCRIPTURE OF THE DAY

Ephesians. 5:16 *"Redeeming the time, because the days are evil."* (NKJV)

Psalm 126:4 *"Bring back our captivity, O LORD, As the streams in the South."* (NKJV)

EXHORTATION

An opportunity is a favorable time or occasion when we have the power to make a decision that will cause a positive change in our lives. It can be described as a gift from the Lord. It is important to recognize that '*Missed*' and '*Lost*' are small words with big meanings. To miss something is failure to be on time while the word '*loss*' means to no longer have something that one once had.

An opportunity is an opening, a favorable circumstance, an advantageous situation, a chance, a room and/or a discovered avenue for profiting. It is that big break, a possibility, a prophetic message delivered to you, etc.

Proverbs 12:27 *"The lazy man does not roast what he took in hunting, But diligence is man's precious possession."* (NKJV)

God's best gift to us is not in 'things' but in opportunities. Blind Bartimaeus got an opportunity, so did the woman with the issue of blood who got healed by Jesus. People who are highly successful are opportunity-grabbers; if you dismiss an opportunity, you will most likely end up unsuccessful.

Some opportunities are short lived, once missed or lost, it is gone forever! It may never be found again; opportunities should not be taken lightly. Most often than not, it is the enemy's way of stealing our blessing. However, it's not all gloomy as opportunities can be regained by praying the right prayers. Examples of opportunities a man or woman can miss are:

- An opportunity to give their life to JESUS
- An opportunity to learn new things
- An opportunity to make money

■ An opportunity to get married in good time

If you have lost any of the opportunities mentioned here or not, I am glad to tell you, you are recovering all today!

CONFESSION
Isaiah 60:1
"Arise, shine; for thy light is come, and the glory of the Lord is risen upon thee."

PRAYER POINTS
1. Lord, I thank you for daily loading me with opportunities and benefits. Thank you for remaining faithful to your word over my life.
2. Father, I thank you for all the life changing opportunities you brought my way last year and the ones to come in 2024.
3. Father, glorify yourself in me. Let every one of my lost opportunities be restored unto me. Where I have failed before, Lord, lift me up with your mighty power in Jesus' name.
4. Lord just like you restored Jacob, let everything that concerns my life be restored.
5. You created me for a purpose, may I fulfill your purpose concerning my life.

6. Father let me find favor in your sight and before men and women. Let them call me the blessed of the Lord.

7. My blessings shall no man take away from me.

8. Father, make me a vessel unto honor even in a foreign land. Let men rise to honor me and be a blessing to me.

9. Every evil manipulation that seeks to make me remain where you have not placed me, Lord let them be destroyed in my life.

10. I escape every trap of the enemy to stop me from grabbing my opportunities.

11. My eyes are opened to see opportunities in 2024.

12. My ears are opened to hear of opportunities in 2024.

DAY 9

PRAYER FOR THE BODY OF CHRIST AND HCC WORLDWIDE

SCRIPTURE OF THE DAY
1 Corinthians 12:27 *"Now you are Christ's body, and individually members of it."*

EXHORTATION

In Ephesians 4:3, we are called to be eager to maintain the unity of the Spirit in the bond of peace. We need to pray for the leaders and shepherds in the body as we are urged in Hebrews 13:17. The church of Christ needs to grow in wisdom, strength and unity. The devil is on an unending mission to divide the body by sowing seeds of discord across denominations. Our prayers for one another are powerful and can bring transformation, healing and unity within the body of Christ. Today, let us raise our voices in intercession for believers in Christ and all HCC churches planted worldwide, for the ever-increasing glory of God and the pulling down of strongholds.

CONFESSION

Matthew 16:18 *"And I say unto thee, that thou art Peter, and upon this rock I will build my church and the gates of hell shall not prevail against it."*

PRAYER POINTS

1. Lord, let unity and love prevail within the body of Christ, that we may be one as Jesus prayed in John 17:21.

2. Lord, send down the revival into our churches.
3. We throw out the net of salvation to draw people from all over the world.
4. Let there be a fresh fire in the body of Christ worldwide.
5. Lord, help us to stay faithful and obedient to your commands in Jesus' name.
6. Lord, strengthen believers spiritually, that they may grow in wisdom, understanding, and knowledge of His word.
7. In HCC, there shall be no record of losses and premature death in Jesus' name.
8. Let chapters of celebration be opened unto us in all HCC branches.
9. Lord, send us burden bearers to support the kingdom work in HCC financially.
10. Fill our services with testimonies in Jesus' name and draw men unto the church because of our testimonies.
11. Lord, cause us to be a sign and wonder to the world.
12. Lord, bring every member of HCC into an encounter with you in Jesus' name.

DAY 10

OPENED HEAVENS

SCRIPTURE OF THE DAY

Psalm 24:7-10 *"Lift up your head, O ye gates; and be ye lift up, ye everlasting doors; and the King of glory shall come in. Who is this King of glory? The LORD strong and mighty, the LORD mighty in battle. Lift up your heads, O ye gates; even lift them up, ye everlasting doors; and the King of glory shall come in. Who is this King of glory? The LORD of hosts, he is the King of glory."*

EXHORTATION

As believers, we operate under open heavens and are qualified for it in all spheres of our lives. In view of this, be expectant of open heavens, ready to pour down blessings and God's goodness upon us. Picture in your mind the heavens wide open, ready to release an abundance of favor, grace, and divine provision. I pray that the opened heavens become a gateway for God's goodness to flood into your life. Trust that as you align your heart with His, the divine favor will transform your circumstances, bringing forth joy, peace, and a profound sense of His abiding presence.

This 30-day journey is not just about abstaining from certain things but about positioning ourselves to receive the overflowing goodness that God desires to lavish upon His children. May you walk in the assurance that the heavens are open wide, ready to shower you with blessings beyond measure.

CONFESSION

Luke 3:21 *"Now when all the people were baptized, it came to pass, that Jesus also being baptized, and praying, the heaven was opened."*

PRAYER POINTS

1. Holy Spirit, activate my spiritual womb for conception in Jesus' name.
2. Holy Spirit, activate my spiritual wings to fly like an eagle in Jesus' name.
3. Holy Spirit, activate my hands to prosper this year in Jesus' name.
4. Holy Spirit, activate my feet to possess the land in the name of Jesus.
5. Holy Spirit, activate my eyes to see the glory

of God.

6. Holy Spirit, activate my ears to hear in the spirit.

7. Holy Spirit, activate my heart to receive wisdom and understanding in Jesus' name.

8. Holy Spirit, activate my soul to receive divine knowledge in Jesus' name.

9. Holy Spirit, activate my mouth to prophesy with fire in Jesus' name.

10. Holy Spirit, activate my body for divine healing in Jesus' name.

11. Holy Spirit, activate my hands to war and my fingers to fight in Jesus' name.

12. Holy Spirit, activate my body, soul and spirit for revival in Jesus' name.

DAY 11

LET MY FINANCIAL GATE OPEN

SCRIPTURE OF THE DAY

Isaiah 60:11 *"Therefore thy gates shall be open continually; they shall not be shut day nor night; that men may bring unto thee the forces of the Gentiles, and that their kings may be brought".*

EXHORTATION

In the natural realm, gates are used for security and protection. In the spiritual realm, God uses gates –which you can't see with your physical eyes like you can see the gate of your house – to secure, protect and fortify people's lives.

There are spiritual gates controlled by the devil. These evil spiritual gates existed in the time of Abraham and others in the Bible. (**Genesis 22:17**). Gates serve as entry points; entry points to a house (**Luke 16:20**), city (**1 Kings 17:10**), palace (**Esther 5:13**), church (**Acts 3:2**), or a person's life (**Isaiah 60:11**). Similarly, by unseen entry points, the devil sends sin, problems, afflictions and all manner of evil into people's lives.

God promised us in Isaiah 45:2-3 that *"I will go before you and make the crooked places straight, I will break in pieces the gates of bronze and cut the bars of iron; I will give you the treasures of darkness and hidden riches of secret places, that you may know that I, the Lord, who call you by your name, am the God of Israel."*

God needs to clear the way for you to be able to take delivery of the treasures of darkness and hidden riches of the secret place; until the gates of brass are pulled down, there will not be any secret riches.

CONFESSION

Deuteronomy 14:29 *"And the Levite, (because he hath no part nor inheritance with thee,) and the stranger, and the fatherless, and the widow, which [are] within thy gates, shall come, and shall eat and be satisfied; that the LORD thy God may bless thee in all the work of thine hand which thou doest."* **(KJV)**

PRAYER POINTS

1. O Lord, let my gates of divine blessings open as from today in Jesus' name.
2. Power to enter into my gates of blessings come upon me now in Jesus' name.
3. Strong man standing at the gates of my destiny, fall down and die in Jesus name.
4. Evil monitors at the entrance of my gates of blessing, scatter now in Jesus' name.
5. O Lord, shatter to pieces every gate of bronze; every gate of stagnation erected around my life.
6. O Lord my Father, cut down all bars of iron hindering and resisting my spiritual, financial,

career, educational and marital progress.

7. I declare all round progress to manifest over my life.

8. Father in the name of Jesus Christ; I destroy whatsoever that is used spiritually or physically to shut my door by fire in Jesus' name. (Joshua 6:1)

9. Father in the name of Jesus Christ; every spirit of dryness and closure that has besieged my financial open door to bring me to emptiness, I destroy you now by the power of the blood of Jesus Christ. (2 Kings 6: 24-25)

10. Every gate of death opened before me and my family, waiting for us to walk right in, I shut you up permanently in the name of Jesus.

11. Every meeting held because of me, to cut my life short in its prime, is scattered in Jesus' name.

12. I declare the release of my marriage, husband, wife and children from the hindrance of ancestral gates.

DAY 12

HEAVEN CONSCIOUSNESS

SCRIPTURE OF THE DAY

1 Corinthians 15:19 *"If all our hope is just in this world, we are among men most miserable."*

EXHORTATION

As believers, it is expedient to know that you are an eternal being, a citizen of heaven and made in the likeness of God (Genesis 1:27). Our ultimate destination is heaven, our time here is short; hence, we should not be consumed by the temporal concerns of this world but be heaven-conscious in all that we do. Learn to be vigilant and guard against worldly distractions that may deter you from staying heaven-conscious. The present sufferings are nothing compared to the glory that is above. Let us strive to keep our gaze focused on the things above where our treasures lie. A place where moths cannot destroy and robbers cannot steal from.

CONFESSION

Jude 1:24 *"To him who is able to keep you from stumbling* *and to present you before his glorious presence without fault and with great joy."*

PRAYER POINTS

1. Lord, help me to be bold about salvation so that unbelievers can also take part of it.
2. Lord, help me to view my current situation in the light of eternity.
3. I bring down everything that exalts itself against God in my heart and I enthrone God as the King of my heart.
4. Lord, search my heart for whatever doesn't look like you and take it away in Jesus' name.
5. Lord, help me to be content in whatever you give me and in godliness.
6. Lord, continue to keep me in your perfect will.
7. Empower me to preach the gospel as you mandated me.
8. Lord, continue to lead me on the path of righteousness all the days of my life.
9. Lord, work on my eyes and heart to remain fixed on you always.
10. I pray that the eyes of my understanding be enlightened to know the hope of your calling.
11. I take away every distraction in my walk this

year.

12. Thank you for the gift of eternal life, O Lord.

DAY 13

VICTORY OVER THE SPIRIT OF DEPRESSION

SCRIPTURE OF THE DAY

Proverbs 15:13 *"A merry heart makes a cheerful countenance, but by sorrow of the heart, the spirit is broken".*

EXHORTATION

Depression is a mood disorder that causes a persistent feeling of sadness and loss of interest in your day-to-day activities, making you feel as if life is not worth living. Depression is not just a mood but a spirit-associated infirmity. It is associated with isolation, loneliness, anxiety, rejection, stress, extreme sadness and so much more. There are many who are hiding behind their phones going through deep depression. It is one of the most prevalent things every young adult is going through. This will not be your portion. You have a sound mind and Spirit.

How to overcome depression?

1.   **Meditate on God's Word:** There is nothing as powerful as the Word of God. So, paste God's words on your walls and confess the words you are hearing.

2.   **Listen to worship songs:** In your car, at home, in your office. Create an atmosphere for miracles through Christian music.

3.   **Listen to messages:** Uplifting messages from your pastor and other anointed ministers of God.

4.   **Pray:** It might be difficult, but pray in the Holy Ghost more often.

5.   **Praise God:** He gives beauty for ashes, oil of joy for mourning and the garment of praise for the spirit of heaviness. This truth about God should stir you to praise God.

6.   **Exercise:** You can try walking around your room and house or go to the gym and jog.

7.   **Ventilate your room:** Allow some natural light in your room, perfume it and lay on your bed. Look at yourself in the mirror and say to yourself —you are unique and God favors you.

Others would include; Count your blessings, think positively, confide in the right people, keep God's law and eat well.

CONFESSION

Isaiah 61:3 *"And provide for those who grieve in Zion — to bestow on them a crown of beauty instead of ashes, the oil of gladness instead of mourning, and a garment of praise instead of despair. They will be called oaks of righteousness, a planting of the Lord for the display of his splendor."*

PRAYER POINTS

1. Arrows of depression fired into my life and backfire in Jesus name.
2. Every cloud of depression over my life and destiny, fade away in Jesus name.
3. Every weapon of depression against me; I decree against you, you will not prosper.
4. Every stranglehold of depression on me, I break you today.
5. Every satanic ministration from the pit of hell bringing depression into my life; expire by fire in Jesus name.
6. Every voice of the enemies speaking depression into mind, I silence you in Jesus

name.

7. Agents of depression programmed around my life and destiny, be consumed by fire in Jesus name.

8. Every dream of depression affecting my life; be canceled.

9. Any sickness in my body as a result of depression; be terminated in Jesus name.

10. Arrows of confusion, clouds of confusion, messages of confusion operating in my life; backfire in Jesus name.

11. I am free from the spirit of depression.

12. I will testify to the goodness of God in my life.

DAY 14

DIVINE SURPRISES FOR THE NEW YEAR –1

SCRIPTURE OF THE DAY

Ephesians 3:20 *"God can do anything, you know—far more than you could ever imagine or guess or request in your wildest dreams! He does it not by pushing us around but by working within us, his Spirit deeply and gently within us."*

EXHORTATION

It is common for a person to feel down and hopeless about a new year. It is not everyone who shouts *"Happy New Year"* that is euphoric about the new year. Not everyone has it all figured out; there are people who are hopeless about enjoying anything *new* in the year because of what the previous year(s) has shown them.

If you are in that category —or not, I have good news for you. The Lord has packages of divine surprises for you. Our God specializes in impossibilities. Abraham was in a hopeless situation; his wife was barren, and his body was also dead. Everything was *"against hope,"* yet he *"believed in hope (Romans 4:18-21)."* This year is just starting, and God is able to give you a mega testimony even as a beginning-of-the-year blessing.

Pray these prayers with all your heart, it will position you for divine surprises before the end of the year, in Jesus' name.

CONFESSION

Isaiah 43:19 *"Behold, I will do a new thing; now it shall* *spring forth; shall ye not know it? I will even make a way in the wilderness, and rivers in the desert."* **KJV**

PRAYER POINTS

1. Oh Lord, thank you for preserving me to see the beginning of 2024. Father, I desire beginning of the year blessings, and testimonies in Jesus' name.

2. Father, surprise me with testimonies over every long-awaited issue in my life and family.

3. Father, let there be total restoration of lost opportunities, blessings, connections, and helpers in Jesus' name.

4. I call forth unexpected resources, opportunities, help and helpers from the North, South, East, and West in Jesus name.

5. I break the powers of territorial powers delaying, and postponing my heaven-ordained blessings for 2024, in Jesus' name.

6. There shall be no carryover of every good thing that God has destined for my life and family in 2024. I decree, let there be a release of these blessings wherever they are hidden in Jesus' name.

7. Lord, I desire strange help, strange provision, strange testimonies this Month in Jesus

name.

8. I forbid the agenda to kill, steal and destroy, there shall be no evil in this month in Jesus' name.

9. You strong man, standing at the gate of my testimony, be wasted in Jesus' name.

10. I destroy every vow of the enemy, witchcraft curses, and ancestral covenants fighting my end of the year celebration in Jesus' name.

11. My family members and I become a candidate for divine surprises in 2024 in Jesus' name.

12. Thank God for answers to your prayers.

DAY 15

DIVINE SURPRISES FOR THE NEW YEAR -2

SCRIPTURE OF THE DAY

2 Kings 7:18 *"It happened just as [Elisha] the man of God had spoken to the king, saying, "Two measures of barley will be sold for a shekel and a measure of finely-milled flour for a shekel tomorrow about this time at the gate of Samaria."* **AMP**

EXHORTATION

Elisha's prophetic declaration of a 24-hour turnaround was unrealistic and impossible to some, but with the power of God, the impossible became possible. As we begin the new year, it is important to never underestimate what God can do. Money answer to all things, and the lack of it can lead to disgrace, servitude, premature death, stagnation, and an inability to fulfill destiny. To fulfill your divine purpose and reach the next level, financial stability is a must. Today, be ready to receive a divine financial surprise within the next 24 hours, as God's blessings pour out upon you in Jesus' name.

CONFESSION

Philippians 4:19 *"And my God will liberally supply (fill until full) your every need according to His riches in glory in Christ Jesus."* **AMP**

PRAYER POINTS

1. By the blood of Jesus, I destroy any strange covenant in my bloodline fighting my financial stability and breakthrough in Jesus' name.

2. Father, connect me to new financial opportunities, and resources, for my next level in Jesus' name.

3. Let my heavens be opened for fresh ideas, and new insights, that will generate millions and billions of monies for me in Jesus' name.

4. Father, I ask for uncommon miracles for the settlement of my debts and other financial responsibilities that I need to settle this year in Jesus' name.

5. Father, by your divine power let my life experience the miracle of divine surprises this month, in the name of Jesus.

6. Father, speedily perform the good things that you have promised me this year, in Jesus' name.

7. Father, bless me greatly this month so that I can be a major kingdom financier in Jesus' name.

8. Oh Lord, according to Isaiah 45:3, I desire that you will give me treasures of darkness, and hidden riches of secret places in Jesus' name.

9. Father, endow me with the required mental ability and wisdom to interpret every opportunity that comes my way correctly and

take maximum advantage of them in Jesus' name.

10. I break the strongholds of debt, bad investments, loss, and poverty over my life and family in Jesus' name. I shall enter into the new year with wealth in Jesus' name.

11. O God, from now on, come and do all things well for me and my household; surprise us beyond measure in the name of Jesus.

12. O God, by your power come and do wonderful and terrible things in my life, surprise me with an uncommon miracle in the name of Jesus.

DAY 16

PRAYER FOR THE NATION

SCRIPTURE OF THE DAY

Jeremiah 29:12-14 *"Then shall ye call upon me, and ye shall go and pray unto me, and I will hearken unto you. And ye shall seek me, and find me, when ye shall search for me with all your heart. And I will be found of you, saith the LORD: and I will turn away your captivity, and I will gather you from all nations, and from all places wither I* *have driven you, saith the LORD; and I will bring you again into the place whence I caused you to be carried away captivity."*

EXHORTATION

We have a unique responsibility to intercede on behalf of our country, whether your place of residence or birth; seeking God's guidance, protection and transformation. Prayer is a powerful tool that can bring about significant changes in the course of our nation. Our nations are under a siege and the devil has his minions planted everywhere. The growth of a nation lies largely in the hands of the believers in it.

Let us pray for unity and reconciliation among the diverse communities within our nation (Ephesians 4:3). As we pray, let us not forget the marginalized in the society —the poor, the oppressed, the orphaned, and the widows.

CONFESSION

2 Chronicles 7:14 *"If my people, which are called by my name, shall humble themselves, and pray, and seek my face, and turn from their wicked ways; then will I hear from heaven, and will forgive their sin, and will heal their land."*

PRAYER POINTS

1. We speak the peace of God over our nation and the rulers.

2. We repent from every shortcoming that has put this nation in jeopardy.

3. Lord, draw us closer to you as a nation, that we may seek your face in prayer and obedience.

4. My God, grant our leaders divine wisdom, discernment and integrity in their governance.

5. Lord, direct our leaders to make godly decisions that align with your principles and promote justice and righteousness.

6. Father, heal the communities in our nation and break down the walls of division in Jesus' name.

7. By the blood of Jesus, we ransom our nation from every power that wants to destroy her destiny.

8. Father, protect our nation from harm, external threats and calamities that may destabilize us.

9. O Lord, let there be a spiritual awakening in our nation that many hearts may turn to you and experience your saving grace.

10. By the blood of Jesus, our nation is delivered from every form of illegality.
11. We decree that our dignity is restored as a nation in Jesus' name.
12. Thank you, Lord, for you have established our nation in righteousness.

DAY 17

OPENED DOORS FOR EXPLOIT

SCRIPTURE OF THE DAY

Isaiah 22:22: *"I will place on his shoulder the key to the house of David; what he opens no one can shut, and what he shuts no one can open."*

EXHORTATION

Great things are not done in secret —they are done in the open. Just as a candle is not lit only to be put under a bushel, the exploits the Lord will do with and through your life will not be a secret in 2024. To actualize this, there must be an opened door of mercy, blessing, connections, prosperity and advancements.

I pray against every evil hand shutting the door God has opened for you to be cut off by fire in Jesus' name.

CONFESSION

1 Corinthians 16:9: *"Because a great door for effective work has opened to me, and there are many who oppose me."*

PRAYER POINTS

1. O Lord, open the door of my joy and divine connection for me, in the name of Jesus.
2. My Father, cut off the evil hands closing my destiny doors against me, in the name of Jesus.
3. O Lord, make a way for me this year where there is no way in Jesus' name.
4. I use the key of David to open the doors of my blessings, marriage, finances, promotion etc., in Jesus' name.
5. Let the power of God remove the satanic gateman preventing my freedom and opportunity from getting to me, in Jesus' name.
6. I speak destruction unto every stubborn situation in my life and command them to

come out by fire, in the name of Jesus.

7. O ye gates of my prosperity and advancement; be lifted now, in Jesus' name.

8. I command every padlock on my doors of opportunities to break by fire, in Jesus' name.

9. Any strange hand knocking at the doors of my joy in order to attack me and steal my goods, O God, arise and scatter their plans, in Jesus' name.

10. The key to open all the closed doors linking to my job and marital connections; I receive it by fire, in the name of Jesus.

11. O ye doors of favour, prosperity, increase, elevation, success, greatness etc., begin to burst open without any apology, in Jesus' name.

12. Any door of breakthrough that I have been knocking over the years, tonight, open by fire in Jesus' name.

DAY 18

LORD GIVE ME MEN TO SUPPORT MY ASSIGNMENT

SCRIPTURE OF THE DAY

Ezekiel 36:37 *"Thus saith the Lord God; I will yet for this be enquired of by the house of Israel, to do it for them; I will increase them with men like a flock."*

EXHORTATION

One of the ways by which God blesses and increases us is by blessing us with the gift of men. Human resource is one of the easiest ways to get to the top and a major way to access levels far beyond our imagination because men are doors. The man Moses believed he had all it took to keep Israel victorious in the battlefield but it didn't take long before it was clear that without Aaron and Hur, the two men who held his hands, it wouldn't be possible. We all need people in our lives to fulfill our destinies because a journey made in isolation often ends in desolation. Therefore, we need to pray for God to send important men to our destinies. No man is an island. No man can achieve his dreams all alone.

Everything that happens on earth today, happens because of men (humans). Man is the most important entity that exists on earth. One of the blessings of walking with the Holy Spirit is the ability to develop your sense of discernment. Discernment is the spiritual quality of perception – the ability to perceive thoughts and intentions. One of the secrets of a life of victory is the ability to move as the Spirit moves.

There are four things the gift of men bring into one's life:

Firstly, men bring wisdom, ideas and strategies into your life. Secondly, men convey endorsements and opportunities. Thirdly, men grant you access to financial and material resources. Fourthly, men grant you access to impartation and the prophetic realm.

CONFESSION

Psalm 121:1-2 *"I will lift up mine eyes unto the hills, from whence cometh my help. My help cometh from the Lord, which made heaven and earth."*

PRAYER POINTS

1. Lord, send men to support my destiny and purpose in Jesus' name.
2. O Lord, connect me to the people that matters to my next level.
3. Lord let my Jonathan help me to the palace as you did for King David.
4. Every veil covering my life from my helper; be unveiled by the fire of God.
5. Lord, surround me with people who will assist my life to fulfill my prophecy.
6. Lord let me recognize my helper and let my helper recognize me in Jesus' name.
7. At every junction of my destiny in life; Lord send helpers to help my progress.
8. Lord let your fire break the wall of partition between me and everyone assigned to lift up my head.
9. Lord let the force of favor come upon me to connect with my destiny helper.
10. Father Lord, set up and arrange a meeting between me and my helper that will lead to a change of story this season.
11. Let God arrange my remembrance in the heart of my helpers to help me until I succeed in life and destiny.

12. In the year 2024, I will not lack help in any way
     in Jesus' name.

DAY 19

GRACE FOR JOURNEY MERCIES

SCRIPTURE OF THE DAY

Acts 20:15 *"And we sailed thence, and came the next day over against Chios; and the next day we arrived at Samos, and tarried at Trogyllium; and the next day we came to Miletus."*

EXHORTATION

The above scripture is in reference to the successful and safe journeys of Paul and other missionaries with him in their missionary assignment; they were at Chios, Samos, Trogyllium and Miletus and they arrived alive.

What journey will you embark on this year? Regardless of the number of places your feet will touch in 2024, you will arrive alive in Jesus name. The scripture says He will give His Angels charge over you (Psalms 91:11-12) and He will keep you in all your ways when you submit your ways to Him (Proverbs 3:6).

CONFESSION

Psalm 121:8 *"And they that have passed by have not said: The blessing of the Lord be upon you: we have blessed you in the name of the Lord."*

PRAYER POINTS

1. Every power assigned to interrupt my journeys this year, die in Jesus name.
2. God of mercy, move ahead of me in all my journeys in 2024.
3. I shall arrive alive in all my journeys in Jesus name.
4. Father, break any agreement of death, calamity and distress concerning me and my family in Jesus name
5. My exploits will not be hindered in Jesus name
6. Lord, take away every assignment of darkness that will hinder your light in my life in 2024.
7. Lord Jesus, make 2024 a zero affliction and zero sorrow for me and my loved ones.
8. Powers that have swallowed my virtues; vomit them by the decree of the Lord.

9. 2024 is my year of rest and ease on all sides in Jesus name.
10. Every day in this year, I shall move in the direction of the Holy Spirit.
11. My spirit shall be sensitive and discerning in all my journeys this year in 2024.
12. Thank God in advance for your safe return in 2024.

DAY 20

BREAKING THE SHACKLES OF SPIRITUAL SLAVERY

SCRIPTURE OF THE DAY

Jeremiah 28:2 *"This is what the LORD Almighty, the God of Israel, says: 'I will break the yoke of the king of Babylon."*

EXHORTATION

The tale of slavery is an unpleasant one in Africa. Although we have been freed from the shackles of the white men, a lot of people are still heavily under the bondage and shackles of the enemy —the devil.

For some, they might have a good job, good housing and a seemingly good life but it doesn't mean the absence of spiritual slavery and bondage such as depression, anxiety, suicidal thoughts and so on. For others, it is their home, job, children, business that is heavily under the slavery of the devil.

In this 30–Day program, I pray that your spiritual eyes shall be opened to see what part of your life is held by the shackles of spiritual slavery and in Jesus' name. You are victorious over the devil, through the blood of the Lamb. Amen.

CONFESSION

Isaiah 10:27: *"And it shall come to pass in that day, that his burden shall be taken away from off thy shoulder, and his yoke from off thy neck, and the yoke shall be destroyed because of the anointing."*

PRAYER POINTS

1. My foundations; the blood of Jesus Christ is speaking to you, respond now.
2. Ancestral evil dedications; the Blood of the Lamb is speaking to you, respond now.

3. Inherited sins; the blood of Jesus Christ is washing you away.

4. Curses in my ancestral lines; the authority of the word is against you now, break and release me.

5. Ancestral handing-over of my glory; be overturned, be revoked by the blood of Jesus.

6. Sell-outs of descendants by my ancestors; my case is different, I have been redeemed by the blood of Jesus, be reversed now by fire.

7. Inherited ancestral debt be annulled by the blood of Jesus Christ.

8. Spiritual slave masters; Jesus is my new Master, lose your hold from me, die by fire, in the name of Jesus Christ.

9. Chains of spiritual slavery and fetters of spiritual servitude; break and release me by fire, in the name of Jesus Christ.

10. Placental attachments tying me to the ancestral lines; catch fire, in the name of Jesus Christ.

11. Stigma of spiritual slavery and servitude; I peel you off, catch fire, in the name of Jesus Christ.

12. Verdicts of spiritual slavery and servitude; I tear you up in the name of Jesus Christ.

DAY 21

DELIVERANCE OF THE HANDS AND FEET

SCRIPTURE OF THE DAY:

Psalms 22:16 *"For dogs have surrounded me; The congregation of the wicked has enclosed me. They pierced my hands and my feet;"*

EXHORTATION

There are many hands and feet that have been caged. Feet symbolizes journey and movement while hands symbolize prosperity. The wealth of many have been hindered because their hands are tied while some people may find out that they are unable to move to the next level because their feet have been tied. This fasting period is designed to make you move according to the agenda of the Almighty for your life and grab your inheritance for the last quarter of the year.

CONFESSION

Psalms 25:15 *"My eyes are ever toward the LORD, For He shall pluck my feet out of the net."*

PRAYER POINTS

1. My hands reject any object of pollution prepared against me in the name of Jesus.

2. Holy Ghost, anoint my hands and my feet for uncommon testimonies in the name of Jesus.

3. Father, by the power that breaks yokes, let every yoke upon my hands be broken in the name of Jesus.

4. Any handwriting of darkness upon my hands, I wipe you off by the power in the blood of Jesus.

5. I cancel every satanic appointment with failure upon my hands in the name of Jesus.

6. My feet receive the fire to move forward in the name of Jesus.

7. Every authority of darkness, assigned to paralyze my feet, die in the name of Jesus.

8. My feet reject the covenant of backwardness in the name of Jesus.

9. You evil altars, erected against my moving forward, be up-rooted and scatter, in the name of Jesus.

10. Every power of failure at the edge of success, programmed into my feet; die in the name of Jesus.

11. Thou power of poor finishing, programmed into my feet, die in the name of Jesus.
12. Anointing to walk into all round success, come upon my feet in the name of Jesus.

DAY 22

PRAYER FOR BUSINESS AND CAREER PROSPERITY

SCRIPTURE OF THE DAY

Deuteronomy 8:18 *"But remember the LORD your God, for it is he who gives you the ability to produce wealth, and so confirms his covenant, which he swore to your ancestors, as it is today".*

EXHORTATION

You need prayers —whether you are a first-time business owner or you have an existing business. There is need to ask the Lord for patience and wisdom to make the right decisions. You need to pray that the right customers be led to you and that you will rise to the occasion to serve them well.

You need prayers – whether your business is going well, or you'd like to see it grow, or it's stagnating and you'd like to move it forward. God is able to bring you new opportunities, customers, and give you ways of expanding. He is able to give you the wisdom and clarity to recognize the potential, because sometimes, even the simplest things can be blessings in disguise if you know where to look.

You need prayers –when your business is at a crossroad and you need to make some big decisions. It is only by the wisdom of the Lord that you can implement new ideas and make the right choices.

Today, take time to pray for His guidance in terms of change. Put your trust into Him and He will lead you to what is best for your business.

CONFESSION

Daniel 6:3 *"Then this Daniel was preferred above the presidents and princes, because an excellent spirit was in him; and the king thought to set him over the whole realm."*

PRAYER POINTS

1. Lord, help me to scale greater heights of life

in my business endeavors and projects in Jesus' name.

2. My Father, let the Holy Spirit go before me and put all things in my favour to emerge successful in business, in Jesus' name.

3. Oh Lord, expose and destroy every plan of the enemy to bring me failure concerning my business in Jesus' name.

4. God, I receive the grace, anointing to undertake great business projects and emerge with outstanding success in Jesus' name.

5. My heavenly Father, destroy every plan of the enemy designed to make me fall sick before executing my business projects in Jesus' name.

6. Oh Lord, destroy all wicked plans of the enemy to make me miss great business ideas and opportunities in Jesus' name.

7. My Father, make me a person of outstanding success in my business in Jesus' name.

8. My Father, grant me the grace to always emerge successful in all areas of my life in Jesus' name.

9. Oh Lord, I declare as from today, my business will begin to experience uncommon miracles in Jesus' name.

10. Oh Lord, uproot and destroy every barrier of the enemy placed upon my business career in Jesus.

11. Lord, I desire strange help, strange provision, strange testimonies this Month in Jesus name.

12. I destroy every vow of the enemy, witchcraft curses, and ancestral covenants fighting my business breakthrough.

DAY 23

POWER TO LOCATE MY PARTNER (FINDING LOVE)

(A day to intercede for the singles in our church and society)

SCRIPTURE OF THE DAY

Isaiah 34:16 *"Seek ye out of the book of the LORD, and read: no one of these shall fail, none shall want her mate: for my mouth it hath commanded, and his spirit it hath gathered them."*

EXHORTATION

The scripture says *"it is not good for the man to be*

alone" (Gen. 2:18). God delights in the union of His Children. It was His charge to Adam to increase and multiply the earth. The family is the smallest yet most functional unit in the society and it will only do better when the world is filled with couples who are believers.

The devil deeply hates and fights against Christian homes. Hence, he attempts to delay godly singles who are ripe for marriage via traumas, identity crises, ancestral altars, negative patterns and so on. This is why we must pray for divine guidance as we go about our marital adventure and intercede for those who are in this phase of life.

CONFESSION

Jeremiah 29:11 *"For I know the plans I have for you,"* *says the LORD. "They are plans for good and not for* *disaster, to give you a future and a hope."* **(NLT)**

PRAYER POINTS

1. Oh Lord, in the beginning you created them male and female, therefore I decree today that heaven shall locate my help-meet and connect us in Jesus' name.

2. Oh Lord, your word says it is not good that I

am alone, therefore connect me with my help-meet today in Jesus' name

3. Oh Lord, solve my marital problem today and beam your light to show me the way in Jesus' name.

4. It is your command that I leave my father and mother to be joined to my wife/or husband. Father bring this word to pass in my life this month in Jesus' name.

5. Oh Lord! Show me my Isaac/Rebekah today. Connect me with my husband/wife in Jesus' name.

6. Oh Lord, I know that you can do all things, bring forth my marital testimony in Jesus' name.

7. Jesus Christ the son of David, have mercy on me over these issues of my life (mention them) in Jesus' name.

8. Every evil character that may be hindering my marital breakthrough, I uproot you in Jesus' name.

9. Every evil association that may be misrepresenting me before my God ordained spouse I disconnect myself in Jesus name.

10. Every evil pattern of delayed marriage in my family I separate myself in Jesus' name.

11. I come against every spirit of marital disappointment in Jesus' name.
12. Oh Lord, change my location to where I will meet my husband/wife in Jesus' name.

DAY 24

COVENANT OF FRUITFULNESS

(This is the day set aside to intercede for those waiting for miracle baby among us and within our friends and family)

SCRIPTURE OF THE DAY

Genesis 25:21-23 *"And Isaac intreated the Lord for his wife, because she was barren: and the Lord was intreated of him, and Rebekah his wife conceived. And the children struggled together within her; and she said, If it be so, why am I thus? And she went to enquire of the Lord. And the Lord said unto her, Two nations are in thy womb, and two manners of people shall be separated from thy bowels; and the one people shall be stronger than the other people; and the elder shall serve the younger."*

EXHORTATION

One of the devil's agenda is to make sure every godly marriage is attacked —ranging from barrenness, miscarriages, difficulty in childbearing and many others. The Bible says our Lord gives blessings and adds no sorrow; it also charges us to be fruitful, multiply and replenish the earth. I found praying in the word of God as solutions for ending the era of fruitlessness in many marriages. One of the major reasons most marriages cannot multiply and be fruitful is that they are under a curse. A cursed marriage breeds shame and disgrace. I pray that as you spend time with the Lord in prayer today, your womb is opened and your marriage shall be fruitful in Jesus' name.

CONFESSION

Genesis 17:6 *"I will make you exceedingly fruitful, and I will make nations of you, and kings will come forth from you."*

PRAYER POINTS

1. O Lord, in the beginning, your declaration to mankind was to be fruitful, to multiply, and replenish the earth. I stand by your word this day and I declare my fruitfulness in Jesus' name.

2. Our covenant fathers; Abraham, Isaac, and Jacob all had their children, therefore I

declare that I shall have mine in Jesus' name.

3.   O Lord! I declare today that I shall be fruitful and multiply in Jesus' name.

4.   Father visit me today as you did to Sarah and Hannah in Jesus name.

5.   O Lord, under the new covenant, Jesus paid the price for my fruitfulness, therefore I receive my Children today in Jesus' name.

6.   I believe that what man sees as impossible is possible for God in my life. I shall be pregnant and deliver my own baby this year in Jesus' name.

7.   O Lord, I command every fertility related sickness in the body or blood of my wife —whether fibroid, pelvic inflammatory disease (PID), ovarian cyst, fallopian tube blockage, any other chronic STDs or STIs whatever your names are— I command you to disappear from my wife's body in Jesus' name.

8.   O Lord, remove whatever is the root cause of my barrenness today. Make me a mother this month in Jesus' name.

9.   My Father and My God, remember me even as you remembered Rachel and opened her womb, remember me today, listen to me

today and open my womb today in Jesus' name.

10. Oh Lord, bless me today with the blessing of the breasts and of the womb in Jesus' name.

11. I prophesy that there shall be no other miscarriage in my life again in Jesus' name.

12. O Lord, open my eyes to the Solution of my fruitfulness in Jesus name. Amen.

DAY 25

ENCOUNTERING THE HOLY SPIRIT

SCRIPTURE OF THE DAY

Romans 8:26 *"Likewise the Spirit also helpeth our infirmities: for we know not what we should pray for as we ought: but the Spirit itself maketh intercession for us with groanings which cannot be uttered."*

EXHORTATION

Who is the Holy Spirit? He is the executor of the Father's Will. In Genesis 1:1, the scripture speaks of God in the beginning, creating the heavens and the earth. Every human being is created to be dependent and not self-sustained. You are created to fulfill a purpose on earth (Jer. 1:5). You are a spirit with soul and with body; these must be managed equally.

In Genesis 1, all creatures were called out, but God formed man. We are created to depend on the Holy Spirit, the Spirit who moved to create this planet earth. It is impossible to live without the superior Spirit on the earth, else other spirits which are gatekeepers will challenge you. Many things will happen as you ascend in life –it is important to do life with the Spirit.

The way forward is to develop intimacy with the Holy Spirit. If you depend on your intelligence, it is not enough to take you there. In a thriving relationship with the Holy Spirit; barriers are broken, communities are formed, differences are ditched, unity is established, disease is cured, health is restored, addiction is broken, homelessness is removed, cities are renewed, races are reconciled, hope is revived, people are blessed, businesses prosper, finances are restored, jobs are provided, and church stays alive, vibrant, and thriving like never before.

Not through your human abilities and cleverness can you navigate your destiny here on earth.

Proverbs 3:5 *"Trust in the LORD with all your heart, And lean not on your own understanding."* (NKJV)

When the Holy Spirit takes over, He changes everything. Nothing stays the same. Will you let Him?

CONFESSION

2 Corinthians 3:5-6 *"Not that we are competent in ourselves to claim anything for ourselves, but our competence comes from God. He has made us competent as ministers of a new covenant—not of the letter but of the Spirit; for the letter kills, but the Spirit gives life."* (NIV)

PRAYER POINTS

1. Lord, ignite in me a deep desire to know you.
2. Holy Spirit, I open my heart completely to you. I surrender all that I am to your hands.
3. Holy Spirit, fill me anew today with fresh power and grace.
4. Grant me heightened sensitivity to discern your voice and leading in 2024.
5. Holy Spirit, activate and release the spiritual

gifts within me. May they operate for the common good and the advancement of Your kingdom.

6. I pray for a fresh anointing to serve You and others effectively. Empower me to be a vessel of Your love, grace, and power in the places You have planted me.

7. Holy Spirit, draw me into a deeper intimacy with the Father and the Son. Help me to know and experience the love that surpasses all understanding.

8. Grant me Your wisdom and discernment. Guide my decisions, actions, and choices, so they align with Your perfect will for my life.

9. Holy Spirit, teach me to pray in alignment with God's heart. Lead me into a breakthrough in prayer, and may my intercession be powerful and effective.

10. Work within me, Holy Spirit, to transform my character. Let the fruit of the Spirit – love, joy, peace, patience, kindness, goodness, faithfulness, gentleness, and self-control – manifest in my life.

11. Holy Spirit, spark a revival within my heart. Fan into flames the passion for You, for Your

Word, and for sharing the gospel with those around me.

12. Empower me with boldness and courage to be a witness for Christ. Let Your presence embolden me to share the good news and make disciples in every sphere of influence.

DAY 26

STRANGE POSSIBILITIES FOR GREAT EXPLOITS

SCRIPTURE OF THE DAY
Psalm 136:6

To him that stretched out the aearth above the waters: for his mercy endureth for ever.

EXHORTATION

One of the most profound verses in the book of Psalm is found in Psalms136:6 which expounds God's awesomeness thus; *"To him that stretched out the earth above the waters, for his mercy endureth for ever"*.

Take a moment to imagine the whole earth, with all its weight and spread, is sitting over waters!

God made it so. It is a strange possibility; the first chapter of Genesis speaks of the strange possibilities embedded in God. Have you stopped to think of how God did not make heaven and the earth from any prepared template or outline? He spoke everything into being! Strange isn't it? Strange possibilities are realities of imagination, penetration and concentration—and even more, an avenue to do exploits. God used all these in all that He created; He did it by His Spirit. Imagination is traveling into the future before you get there; it is sending the soul on an errand and working on the fruits by faith. Penetration is about using keen insight and intuition to perceive a reality and concentration is the energy and profit of focus. Every possibility is at the center of every concentration.

Job 32:8 *"But there is a spirit in man: and the inspiration of the Almighty giveth them understanding."*

What are some examples of possibilities that led to exploit by God in the Bible?

1.   Esther, a slave girl who became a first lady in a foreign nation. (Esther 2:17)

2.   David, a little shepherd boy killed a war General in a battle with only one sling and one stone. (1 Samuel 17:42-51)

3.   Nehemiah, a mere cup bearer in a palace, mobilized to rebuild the fallen walls of Jerusalem and he achieved it in 52 days! (Nehemiah 6:15)

4.   Joshua prayed and commanded the sun and moon to stand still for 24 hours and it was so. (Joshua 10:12-14)

The scriptures are filled with several other strange possibilities. Can God fulfill strange possibilities in your life? Yes, He can!

How will God do all these for you? He will do it by His spirit. Hear what the Bible says in Romans 8:11: *"But if the Spirit of him that raised up Jesus from the dead dwells in you, he that raised up Christ from the dead shall also quicken your mortal bodies by his Spirit that dwelleth in you"*.

The Holy Spirit is a spirit of possibilities. Jesus rose from the dead by the Spirit of God. The same spirit is able to empower you to do exploit in His name.

CONFESSION

Luke 18:17 *"But He said, "The things that are impossible with people are possible with God."*

PRAYER POINTS

1. Spirit of life and grace, blessed be your wonderful name.
2. Father, open my life to the expanse of your possibilities in Jesus' name.
3. By your right hand Lord, lift me from my heights into your own heights in Jesus' name.
4. Father, command the earth to yield all its increase into my life in Jesus' name.
5. By your strange acts Lord, change my candlelight to sunlight in Jesus' name.
6. Father, upgrade my stool into a throne in Jesus' name.
7. I receive grace to sit with elders at the gate in Jesus' name.
8. I possess the heritage of my enemies and occupy the territories of my adversaries in Jesus' name.
9. Lord Jesus, flood my spirit with the overflow of your own Spirit in Jesus' name.
10. Power of long-range focus and planning, fall upon me in Jesus' name.

11. Holy Spirit, empower me to challenge myself and exceed my limits in Jesus' name.

12. Spirit of life, capture my future into my present situations in Jesus' name.

DAY 27

CRUSHING STUBBORN OBSTACLES

SCRIPTURE OF THE DAY
Study **Exodus 14**

EXHORTATION
Obstacles are hindrances set by the enemy to stop advancement in life and career. Many destinies have been stopped; marriages that are supposed to be celebrated have been put on hold. The scripture speaks of Apostle Paul in Thessalonians 2:18 where he was going to visit the brethren there but he was hindered by Satan.

Stubborn obstacles may be in the form of curses, negative covenant or even ignorance. They are stumbling blocks to what God has in store for His Children. In this fasting program, you will crush stubborn obstacles hindering you in Jesus name.

CONFESSION

1 Thessalonians 2:18 *"Wherefore we would have come unto you, even I Paul, once and again; but Satan hindered us."*

PRAYER POINTS

1. Everything that must go for me to move forward, go by fire, in the name of Jesus

2. Herod, Goliath, Cain and Pharaoh in my company, scatter, in the name of Jesus.

3. Words of witchcraft, attacking my star, fall down and die, in the name of Jesus.

4. Rivers of iniquity, coming down from my generation, I stop you before you stop me, in the name of Jesus.

5. Angels of war; pursue those holding what belongs to me and command them to release it, in the name of Jesus.

6. Every roaring lion that has vowed to devour me, die, in the name of Jesus.

7. Every instrument of wickedness assigned against me, backfire, in the name of Jesus.

8. My stolen oil, hear the word of the Lord; gather back to my head, in the name of Jesus.

9. Every power withholding my instruments of advancement, die, in the name of Jesus.

10. Arrows of shame, backfire in the name of Jesus.

11. Every altar, planning my demotion, die in the name of Jesus.

12. Voices speaking against my rising up, shut up in the name of Jesus.

DAY 28

COMMANDING DIVINE ESCAPE

SCRIPTURE OF THE DAY

Job 1:17 *"While he was still speaking, another messenger came and said, "The Chaldeans formed three raiding parties and swept down on your camels and made off with them. They put the servants to the sword, and I am the only one who has escaped to tell you!"*

EXHORTATION

In scripture, we see that Job suffered many calamities but somehow a person always escaped to tell the story. David who killed Goliath was almost killed by one of the sons of the giant in another battle but he escaped (2 Samuel 21;16-17). You too will escape from evil attacks of the enemy.

The scripture reads in Psalm 124: 6-8 *"Blessed be the Lord, who hath not given us as a prey to their teeth. Our soul is escaped as a bird out of the snare of the fowlers: the snare is broken, and we are escaped. Our help is in the name of the Lord, who made heaven and earth."*

In the same Psalm 124, we read of fowlers and their snares; fowlers were professional bird-catchers in the days before firearms; they captured birds by spreading a net on the ground and attaching it to a springed trap or snare. The book of Jeremiah 45:5b reads *"For I will bring disaster on all people, declares the Lord, but wherever you go I will let you escape with your life."*

There is no doubt we live in very dangerous times. Economic experts, scientific experts and even spiritual seers are all predicting very difficult times ahead in 2024. I write to you on the authority of Christ that God will give you a divine escape from death, debt, failure, bad health, calamity, accident, diseases and plagues, evil plots against you, and chaos in Jesus' name. This is not for you alone but for many that belong to your household and those connected to you.

Such times happened in the Bible and the widow of Zarephath was divinely saved from debt, shame, poverty, loss and emptiness within 24 hours. God divinely made Mordecai and the Jews escape from destruction and death at the hands of Haman. Daniel divinely escaped from the lion's den while the three Hebrew brothers divinely escaped from the burning fiery furnace. As much as these examples are great, we are to remember that the greatest divine escape through the salvation of our soul, is escaping from the wrath of hellfire which was divinely designed for Satan and his cohorts.

CONFESSION

Proverbs 11:21 *Assuredly, the evil man will not go unpunished, but the descendants of the righteous will be delivered"*.

PRAYER POINTS

1. Every attempt of sudden death made against me be aborted in Jesus' name.

2. Arrows of untimely death fired into my life, backfire by Holy Ghost fire to the senders in Jesus' name.

3. I withdraw my name and that of my family from the register of untimely death in Jesus' name.

4. I refuse to be mistaken for evil in Jesus' name.

5. Satanic grave dug for me and my family, swallow your diggers in Jesus' name.

6. I escape every deadly trap set for me by the enemy.

7. My career, business and family shall escape every tragedy in 2024.

8. Every altar sponsoring evil in my ancestral lineage, I pull you down by fire in Jesus' name.

9. Any weapon fashioned against me in 2024, I disarm you in Jesus' name.

10. My family and I are covered by the blood of Jesus.

11. This year, a thousand shall fall at my side in Jesus' name.

12. Thank you Lord for I have escaped evil traps and demonic attacks.

DAY 29

OIL IN MY LAMP

SCRIPTURE OF THE DAY
Study **Matthew 25:1-13**

EXHORTATION

In this parable, ten virgins took their lamps to meet the bridegroom. The wise ones took oil with them, while the foolish ones did not. As they waited, the bridegroom arrived, and the lamps of the wise virgins filled with oil, shone brightly, allowing them to join in the celebration. The foolish virgins, lacking oil, were unprepared and missed the joyous occasion. As we go forward in the new year, our lives are akin to those lamps. The oil symbolizes the spiritual readiness, wisdom, and preparedness needed for the opportunities, challenges, and encounters that the new year will bring. Here are a few key insights:

- **Spiritual Preparedness**

Just as the wise virgins were prepared with oil, let us move in the new year with spiritual readiness.

Cultivate a deep relationship with God through prayer, meditation, and regular engagement with His Word. This spiritual preparedness acts as the oil that fuels the flame of our faith.

■ Wisdom for the Journey

The oil in the lamps represents the wisdom we gain from God. Seek divine wisdom as you navigate through the uncertainties of the new year. Proverbs 3:5-6 encourages us to trust in the Lord and lean not on our own understanding, acknowledging Him in all our ways.

■ Being Filled with the Holy Spirit

In Zechariah 4:6, we see that it is not by might nor by power, but by the Spirit of the Lord. Allow the Holy Spirit to fill you afresh in this new season. Embrace the guidance, empowerment, and comfort that the Spirit provides.

■ Anointing for the service

The anointing oil used for consecration in the Old Testament reminds us of our consecration to God's service. As we step into the New Year, let us commit ourselves to God's purposes, seeking His guidance and anointing for the tasks ahead.

CONFESSION

Psalm 45:7 *"You love righteousness and hate wickedness; therefore God, your God, has set you above your companions by anointing you with the oil of joy." (NIV)*

PRAYER POINTS

1. Lord, I pray for an intimate connection in this season. Reveal yourself to me, even more.
2. Lord, heighten my spiritual sensitivity in this season.
3. I repent of every sin and shortcomings in my life, in Jesus' name.
4. Lord, bless all my financial endeavors and give me wisdom to manage my resources.
5. By the blood of Jesus, I receive divine health, stability and vitality in Jesus' name.
6. O Lord, let your unity and love envelope my family in Jesus' name.
7. I pray for success, favor and fulfillment in my career and business.
8. Lord, direct and guide me in the matter of my destiny and purpose in Jesus' name.
9. Let there be an increase in impact in my ministry, career and business in Jesus' name.
10. Let your anointing for creativity and innovative ideas flow ceaselessly in my

endeavors.

11. Lord, set my prayer and word altar on fire continuously in Jesus' name.

12. I surrender myself to be used by you O Lord in 2024.

DAY 30

LORD REVIVE MY GLORY

SCRIPTURE OF THE DAY

Psalm 8:5 *"For thou hast made him a little lower than the angels, and hast crowned him with glory and honor."*

EXHORTATION

This prayer session is both preventive and curative. The glory of a man is so important. Even the Almighty God guards it and scripture backs it up in Isaiah 42: 8 that He does not share His glory with anyone. Glory represents the fullness of grace and truth in one's life. Glory adds colors to one's life like Joseph's coat of many colors. Glory is the honor and dignity of a man (Psalm 8: 5). It is the beauty of God in you (Exodus 28:2). It is your divine aura. It is that which draws favor to you.

God gives everyone He created some measure of glory in order to fulfill their destiny. This glory beautifies (Exodus 22:2) and sanctifies (Exodus 29:43). The prayer points below are to revive dead and perverted glory. You must note that there are glory stealers, glory users, glory coverers but you will overcome them in Jesus' name.

CONFESSION

Exodus 33:15 *"And he said, I beseech thee, shew me thy glory."*

PRAYER POINTS

1. O Lord, let your hand of fire touch my glory now.
2. Every Satanic hand manipulating my glory, wither by fire.
3. My glory in captivity, jump out and locate me by fire.
4. Fresh glory of the living God and from heaven, envelope me now.
5. Anybody using my glory, I stop you by fire.
6. My hidden glory, appear now and shine for the world to see.
7. My glory is not for sale any further. If anyone has sold it, I take it back by fire.

8. My marital glory, awake and shine now.
9. My financial glory, awake and shine now.
10. My stolen glory, I recover you back by force and by fire.
11. Light of God, disperse any darkness covering my glory.
12. My glory, begin to speak now.

Author's Contact

Mainland Office:
Solution Arena, 156, Ikorodu Road
Onipanu Bus Stop, Lagos.

Island Office:
Testimony Place, Plot 5, Akiogun Road,
Oniru New Market, Lekki, Lagos.

email:
amosfenwa@hccworld.org,
president@amosfenwaministry.org

website:
www.hccworld.org,
www.amosfenwaministry.org

phone:
+234 (0) 812 511 3314,
+234 (0) 803 338 7124,
+234 (0) 703 727 6477

DR. AMOS FENWA
SENIOR PASTOR & GENERAL OVERSEER

HCC GLOBAL OFFICE
Solution Arena
156, Ikorodu Road
Onipanu Bus Stop, Lagos.
Tel: +2348033004930
Website: www.hccworld.org
Email: holytunderich52@gmail.com
Central Administrator: PASTOR TUNDE RICHARD

LAGOS ZONE, NIGERIA
LAGOS HEADQUARTER
Solution Arena
156, Ikorodu Road
Onipanu Bus Stop, Lagos.
Tel: +2348023097589, +2348063037717
www.hccworld.org
Email: adedeji697@gmail.com
Pastor-in-charge: EMMANUEL ADEDEJI

IKEJA, LAGOS STATE
Royal Family
OLOKUN AYO HOUSE
15 Kudirat Abiola Way,
Middle Floor,
Ojota Bus Stop, Ikeja, Lagos.
Tel: +2347058770510
Email: hccikejachurch@gmail.com
　　　　pastoromojolataiwo@gmail.com
Pastor-in-charge: TAIWO OMOJOLA

LEKKI, LAGOS STATE
Testimony Place
Plot 5, Akiogun Road, by Oniru Market Road,

(Alternative Route A, After Lekki Toll Gate) Lekki,
Lagos.
Tel: +2348175428287, +2348175428290
Email: info@hcclekki.org
Pastor-in-charge: FEMI OKANLAWON

NEWSPRING CHURCH (HCC Youth Expression)
69, Murtala Mohammed Way,
Yaba, Lagos.
Tel: + 2348028398692, + 2348028117178,
Email: davidbankole73@gmail.com
Pastor -in-charge: DAVID BANKOLE

<u>ABUJA ZONE</u>
ZONAL PASTOR: DR AYO TEGBE

APO, FEDERAL CAPITAL, ABUJA
Home of Achievers
Plot 211, Cadastral Zone B14,
Along Apo Mechanic Village road,
Before Shoprite, Dutse District, Abuja
Tel: +2348033117187, +2348035932243
+2348076016672
Email: hgccabuja@yahoo.com
        hccabujachurch@gmail.com
Zonal Pastor: DR AYO TEGBE

LUGBE, FEDERAL CAPITAL TERRITORY, ABUJA
Home of Grace
1st Avenue,
FHA Lugbe,
Behind Royal Rainbow School,
FCT, Abuja.
Tel: +2348100587775, +2348173297803
Email: hcc.homeofgrace@gmail.com
Pastor-in-charge: EZEKIEL FENWA
KUJE, FEDERAL CAPITAL TERRITORY, ABUJA
Home of Overcomers

Nsukka Union Community Hall
Passali Road, Kuje,
Abuja, FCT.
+2347037272221, +2348051634227
Email: sholicios@yahoo.com
Pastor -in-charge: SHOLA ENIOLA

KUBWA, FEDERAL CAPITAL TERRITORY, ABUJA
Home of Abundance
P-PLAZA
Kubwa Extension Layout,
Along NYSC Camp Road,
Opposite Kubwa Village Market,
Off NEPA Road,
Opposite Success Gate Academy,
Kubwa, Abuja, FCT.
Tel: +2348037052702, + 2348079367664
Email: solomonakuboh@gmail.com
Pastor -in-charge: SOLOMON B. AKUBOH

OGBOMOSO, OYO STATE
House of Mercy
Behind Ori-Oke Community High School,
Odo- Alamo, Ogbomoso, Oyo State.
Tel: +2347068483713, +2348066497510
hccogbomoso@yahoo.com
Zonal Pastor: DR AYO TEGBE

UNITED KINGDOM
The Elevation Point
The Elevation Point Building,
3, Herringham Road,
Thames Wharf Barrier Charlton,
London SE7 8NJ
Tel: +447961480394
Email: admin@hgcc.org.uk
Website: www. hgcc.org.uk
Pastor-in-charge: OLUMIDE ADEYILEKA

<u>**UNITED STATES CAMPUSES**</u>
ZONAL PASTOR: DR JOSEPH SIJU

NEW JERSEY
HEADQUARTER
House of Stars
(The Place of Refuge)
1323 Burnet Avenue
Union, NJ 07083
Ph: 844-440-1880, 973 449-3389
Email: info@hccnj.org
         hgpcim@yahoo.com
         jsiju@hccnj.org
Website: www.hccnj.org
 Coordinators: DR JOSEPH & DR. LOLA SIJU

SOUTH JERSEY
Jubilee Place
219 S Burnt Mill Road,
Voorhees, NJ 08043
Tel: +1 862 452 4458, +1 973 489 2615
Email: hccjubileeplace@gmail.com
Coordinators: PASTOR SEYI & PASTOR DORCAS
OLANREWAJU

HOUSTON
HCC light House
Holiday Inn & Suites
25406 Katy Mills Pkwy, Katy, Tx 77494
Contact: +1 713 534 3597
Email: hcclighthouse44@gmail.com
Coordinators:: MIN. LARA & DIMEJI AFOLABI

PENNSYLVANIA
HCC Impact Center
148 Black Oak Ln, McDonald PA 15057
Tel: +1 (862) 766 7994, +1 (347) 869 8819

Email: impacthouse@hccna.church
Coordinators: MIN. FUNSO & MARY ADESANYA

DELAWARE
170 Streamside Circle Unit
2 Smyrna 19977 Delaware
Tel: +1 (908) 265 0449, +1 (862) 588 9944

DALLAS
HCC Newbreed Fellowship
Zoom Meeting Id: 897 0657 8791
Passcode: Refresh
Tel: +1 862 250 1762
Email: dallas@hccna.church
Coordinators: DARE & PELUMI FENWA

INDIANAPOLIS
HCC Fellowship
3526 Aylesford Lane. 46228
Tel: +1 (973) 905 3124
Email: olayanjutoyin66@yahoo.com
Coordinator: MIN. TOYIN AJAYI

NOW OUT

A 400 PAGE
MANUAL CONTAINING
OVER 1,000
PRAYER POINTS

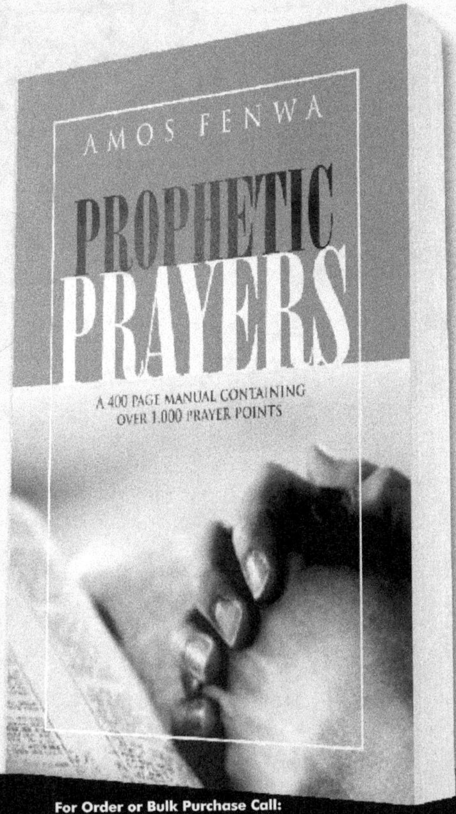

For Order or Bulk Purchase Call:
+234 (0) 703 930 8353, 0809 532 5323
www.amosfenwa.com

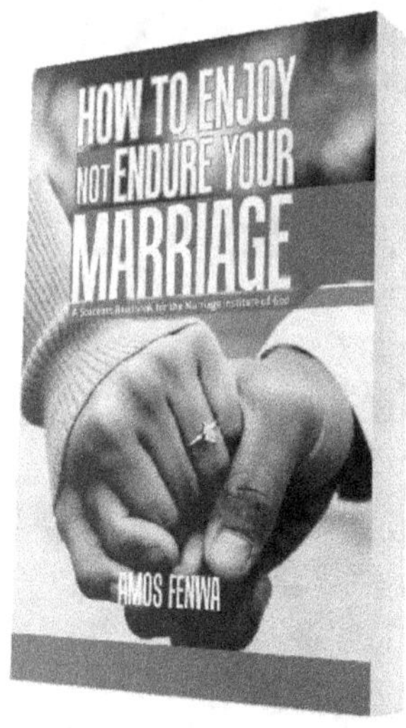

HOW TO ENJOY
NOT ENDURE YOUR
MARRIAGE
AMOS FENWA

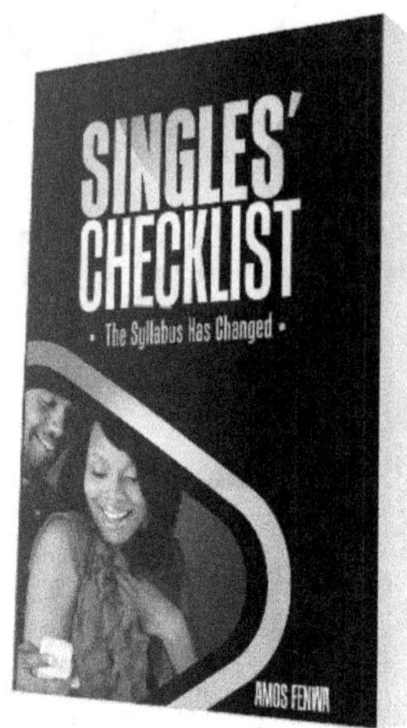

SINGLES'
CHECKLIST
The Syllabus Has Changed
AMOS FENWA

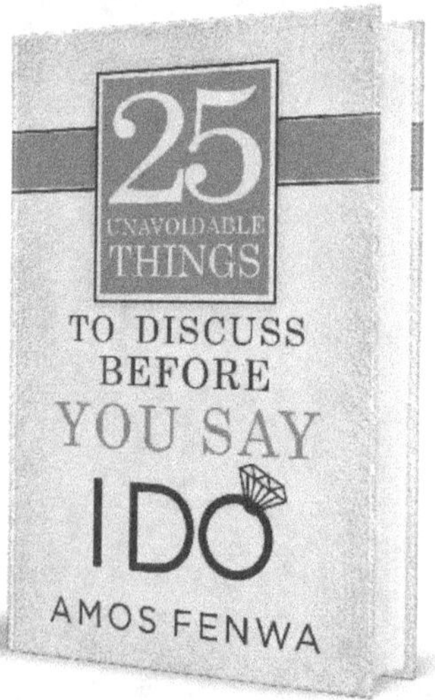

25
UNAVOIDABLE
THINGS
TO DISCUSS
BEFORE
YOU SAY
I DO
AMOS FENWA

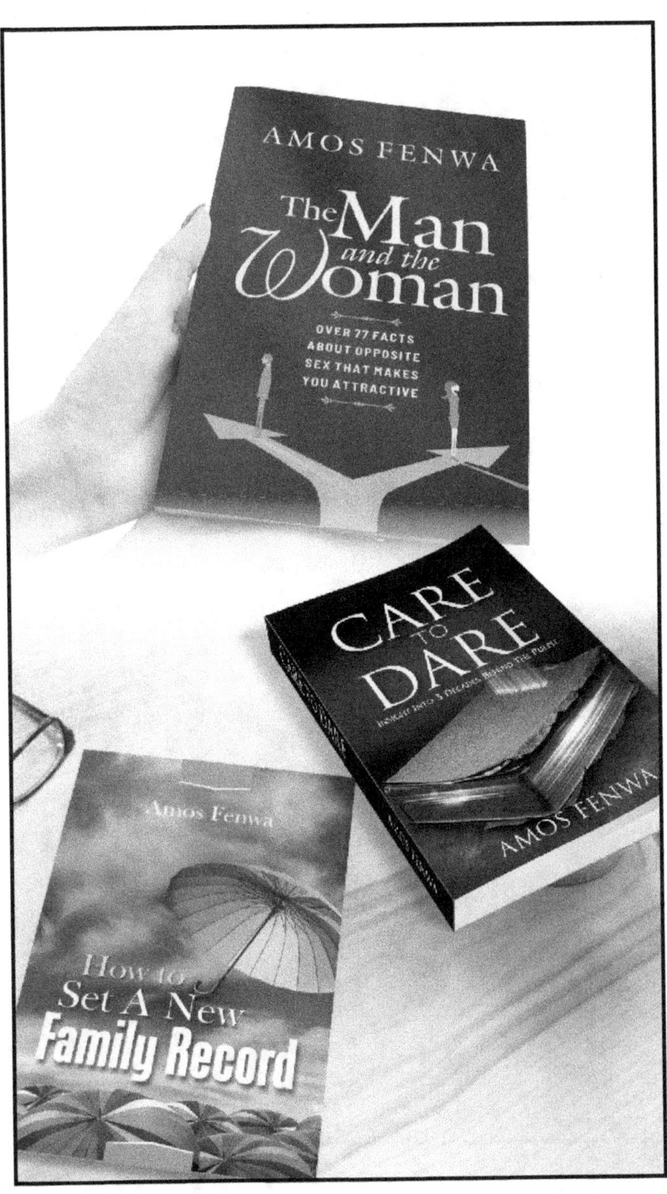

AMOS FENWA
The Man and the Woman
OVER 77 FACTS ABOUT OPPOSITE SEX THAT MAKES YOU ATTRACTIVE
CARE TO DARE
AMOS FENWA
Amos Fenwa
How to Set A New Family Record

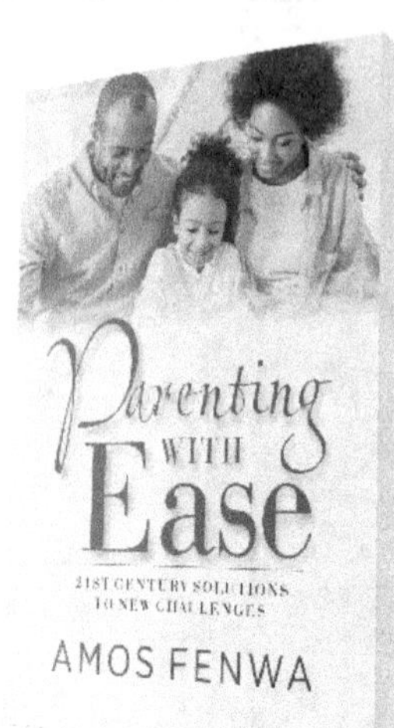
Parenting
WITH
Ease
21ST CENTURY SOLUTIONS
TO NEW CHALLENGES
AMOS FENWA

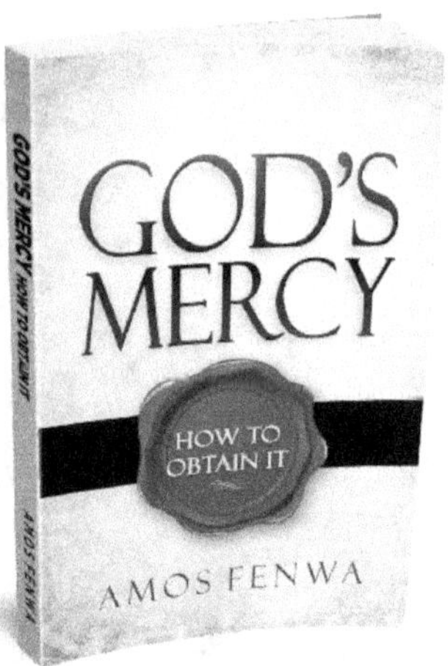
GOD'S MERCY HOW TO OBTAIN IT
GOD'S
MERCY
HOW TO
OBTAIN IT
AMOS FENWA
AMOS FENWA

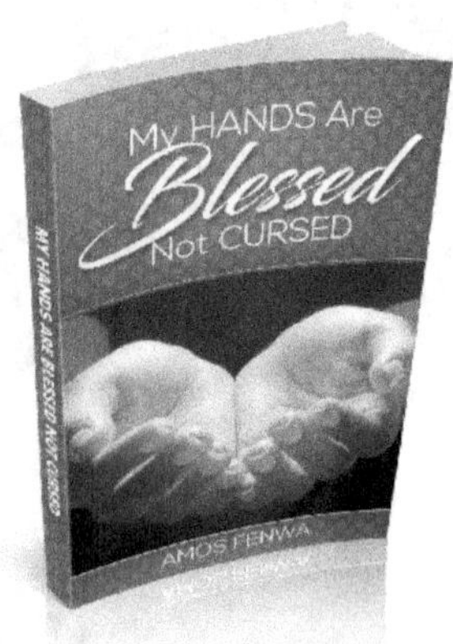
My HANDS Are
Blessed
Not CURSED
MY HANDS ARE BLESSED NOT CURSED
AMOS FENWA

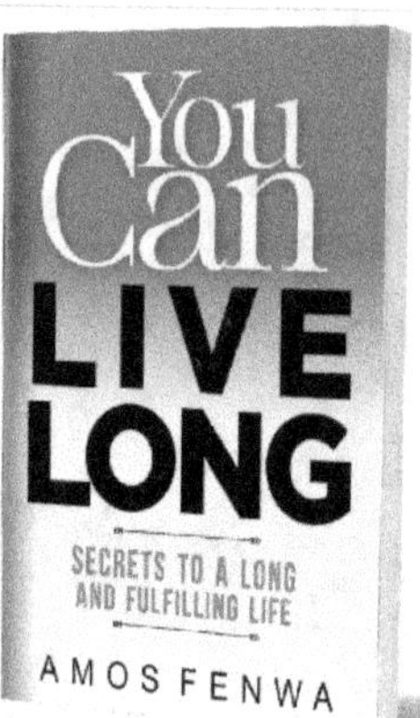
You
Can
LIVE
LONG
SECRETS TO A LONG
AND FULFILLING LIFE
AMOS FENWA

OTHER BOOKS BY
THE AUTHOR

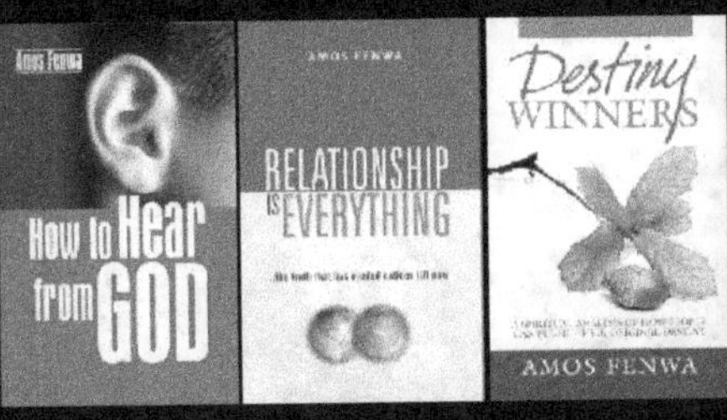

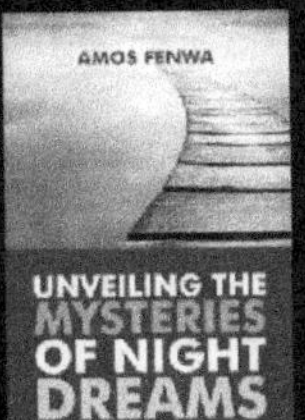

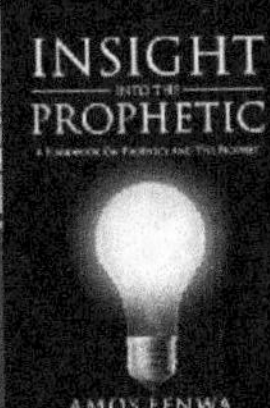

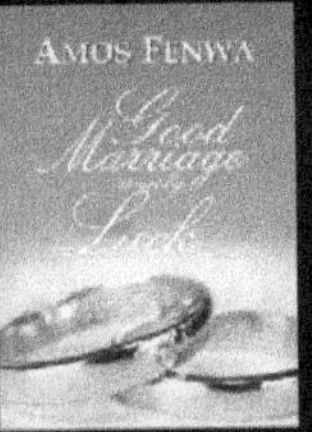

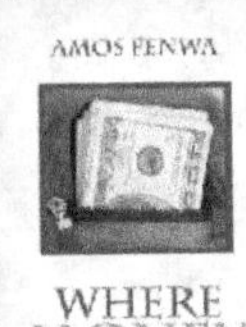

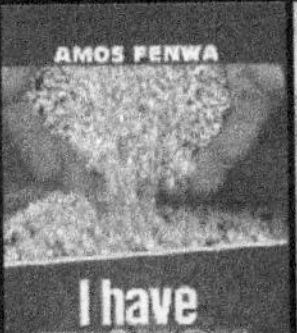

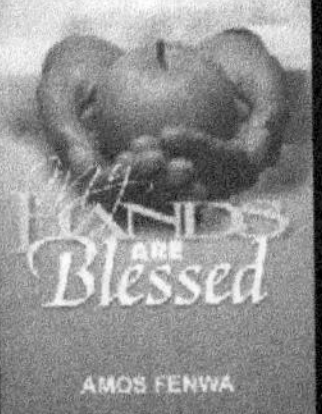

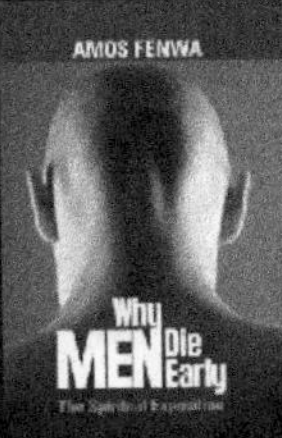

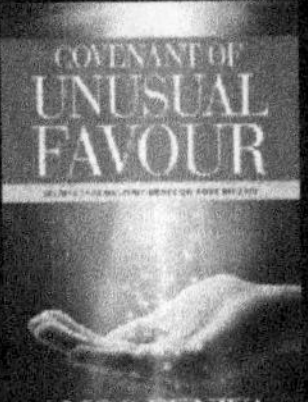

Latest Release

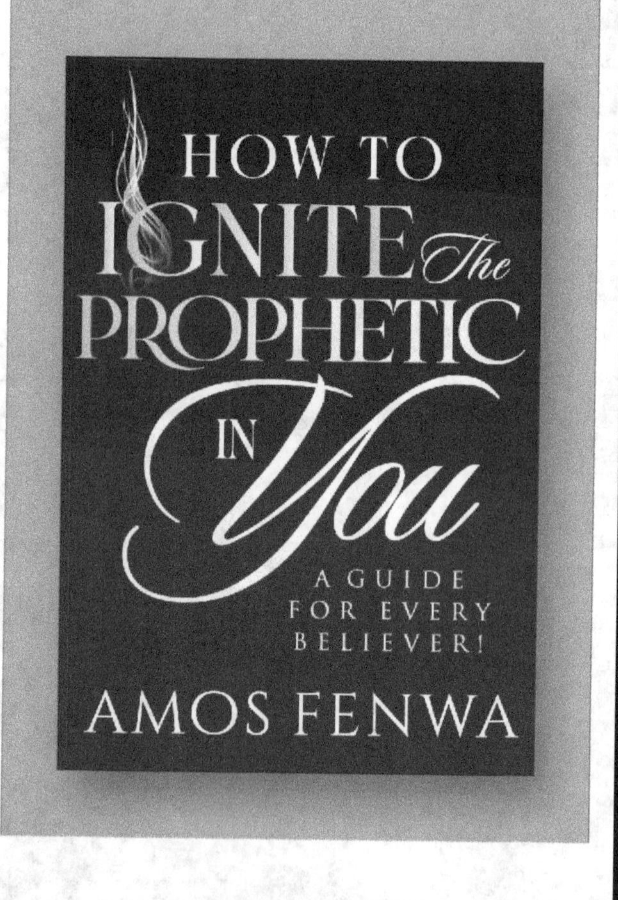